BEV FRANCIS' POWER BODYBUILDING

BEV FRANCIS' POWER BODYBUILDING

By Bev Francis with Bill Reynolds

 Sterling Publishing Co., Inc.   New York
Cassell PLC   London, England

Edited by Laurel Ornitz
Design by Jim Anderson
Selected photos courtesy of Joe Weider,
Publisher, **Flex** *magazine*

Francis, Bev.
 [Power bodybuilding]
 Bev Francis' power bodybuilding / by Bev Francis with Bill Reynolds.
   p.   cm.
 Includes bibliographical references.
 ISBN 0-8069-6909-1
 1. Bodybuilding.   I. Reynolds, Bill.   II. Title.   III. Title: Power bodybuilding.
 GV546.5.F73   1989   89-19735
 646.7′5 — dc20   CIP

Copyright © 1989 by Bev Francis and Bill Reynolds
Published by Sterling Publishing Co., Inc.
387 Park Avenue South, New York, N.Y. 10016
Distributed in Canada by Sterling Publishing
℅ Canadian Manda Group, P.O. Box 920, Station U
Toronto, Ontario, Canada M8Z 5P9
Distributed in Great Britain and Europe by Cassell PLC
Artillery House, Artillery Row, London SW1P 1RT, England
Distributed in Australia by Capricorn Ltd.
P.O. Box 665, Lane Cove, NSW 2066
Manufactured in the United States of America
All rights reserved

CONTENTS

	Introduction	9
1	Bodybuilding Basics	15
2	Power-Bodybuilding Training	41
3	Advanced Bodybuilding Principles	55
4	Effective Bodybuilding Nutrition	81
5	Mind Magic in Bodybuilding	99
6	Contest-Level Bodybuilding Principles	115
7	Pro-Level Bodybuilding Secrets	133
	Appendix: My Favorite Recipes	154
	Index	159

To my husband, Stephen, whose devotion made my transition from World Champion powerlifter to World Champion bodybuilder possible.

And to my parents, Beryl and Fred, who, through the years, have always given me the love and support needed for everything I've done.

ACKNOWLEDGMENTS

All of these people have been instrumental in furthering my athletic career—I want to thank: Joe and Betty Weider; Ben Weider; Mike Neveux; Bill Reynolds; Wayne DeMelia; Gregory and Pam Hines; Jim Manion and Debby Albert; Albert Beckles and Lisa Clark; Jeff and Cory Everson; Gold's Gym/Venice, California (Owners: Pete Grymkowski, Tim Kimber, and Ed Connors); World Gym/Venice (founder and owner: Joe Gold); Sterling Publishing Company (Charles Nurnberg, vice-president); Dr. Bob Goldman; Dr. Arnold Illman; Bob Gruskin; Rochelle Larkin; Ray Rigby; Gael Martin; Roz and Vince Basile; Dr. Al Thomas; Franz Stampfl; Kathy and Ken Leistner; John and Lorraine Francis; Keith and Merylin Francis; George and Jan Francis; John and Jeanette Quinn; Sandy and Vinnie Simmons; Bill McCormick; Howard Briles; and Steve Karel.

In memory of Morty Weinberger   December 3, 1936–August 16, 1984

I represented Oceania (Australia, New Zealand, and the Pacific region) in the shot put at the 1979 World Cup in Track and Field, held in Montreal, Canada.

INTRODUCTION

My outlook on training stems from when I was very young. I learned early that anything really worthwhile has to be worked for—that nothing comes easy. I had four older siblings, and they were all very hard workers. None of them were great athletes, but they were all involved in sports. My oldest brother, for example, used to run about 10 miles a day.

I never imagined that I had what it takes to be a world champion, but I always enjoyed sports. I got a lot of satisfaction from using my body and working hard. Track and field was the sport in which I made my first real achievement.

I had the opportunity to use good facilities and equipment for the first time when I went to college at the age of 19, and I took full advantage of them. I also joined a lot of sports clubs—gymnastics, volleyball, rowing, and track and field.

I had a very good coach in track and field, who said that I had the potential to be a state representative, and that gave me the incentive to work harder. But my main motivation came from wanting to do the best I possibly could.

I started weight training to increase my strength for track and field. I was doing two basic movements: Bench Presses and Squats. After a couple of months, I began making very rapid gains.

As soon as I got used to the movements, it was obvious that I had the potential to develop strength. It felt very natural to me. I got great satisfaction from lifting heavier and heavier weights, and could work very hard. I didn't mind going to the gym, no matter what the weather was or how long I had to stay there. About 3 years after I had begun weight training, I started competitive powerlifting.

At that point, in 1979, I wasn't doing any

Here I am with Arnold Schwarzenegger in Sydney, Australia, in 1980 — the year Arnold made his comeback for his seventh Mr. Olympia title.

bodybuilding training. I was squatting and benching virtually every day, but I didn't know anything about resting or body parts or those sorts of things—and the intensity of my workouts varied. Some days when I benched, I would just go in to the gym and do 5 sets, in an easy pyramid. Other days I'd go in and do 15 sets—hard. I always alternated exercises within a workout, too; I would do one set of Bench Presses and then one set of Squats. I'd sit and rest for a little while, and then do the bench and squat series again. My training was completely unorthodox.

I trained like that for about 5 years. By 1985 I had won six World Powerlifting Championships in a row. After the last one, I decided to concentrate solely on bodybuilding.

My first exposure to bodybuilding came in

early 1983, when I was invited to compete in a physique show in New York City that was being filmed for the *Pumping Iron II—The Women* production. I moved temporarily to New York from my home in Melbourne, Australia, to do specific bodybuilding training. Steve Weinberger was my training partner, and we developed an immediate friendship. I stayed in New York for a couple of weeks after the *Pumping Iron* competition to be with Steve, and then returned to Melbourne. But soon I was back in New York and we were married. Since that time, we have worked together to develop my potential as a bodybuilder, and Steve's influence on me has been tremendous.

Before I flew off to New York to train for the competition, I went to see my good friend Vince Basile in Sydney. Vince owns a local gym, and he was the only bodybuilder I knew then. Both Vince and his wife, Roz, had been encouraging me to switch over from powerlifting to bodybuilding for a long time.

Vince showed me some basic routines, which I worked on until I came to America. Besides that, all I really did was pick up a couple of bodybuilding magazines to learn about the sport and add a few routines to my workout.

I learned quickly that a bodybuilder handles weights very differently from a powerlifter. When you're powerlifting, you want to lift the heaviest possible weight; so, when you think about getting stronger, you're really thinking

This photo was taken in 1981. I'm standing with Sergio Oliva, Mr. Olympic 1967, '68, and '69.

This shot shows me winning the 1983 World Powerlifting Championship. I have never been defeated in any powerlifting contest.

about lifting as much weight as possible. You try to use as much of your body as you can to help you in a particular lift. You concentrate on the weight, not on the muscle or group of muscles being used. The lift is the focus of your energy; you put every physical and mental effort towards lifting the weight.

In bodybuilding, my training is completely different. The weight has now become almost inconsequential. I just choose a weight that gives the muscle the resistance I feel it needs when I do the movement. That weight varies throughout my workouts, although I still use fairly heavy weights.

In bodybuilding, I focus all my attention on a particular muscle. I try to isolate the movement so that the rest of my body is completely still. I try to feel the muscle throughout the entire movement, in contrast to a lot of bodybuilders who think about the weight instead. For instance, when they are doing Pulldowns behind the neck, they're probably thinking about the weight going up and down—they're probably thinking about moving that plate. I don't care where the plate is; what I'm thinking about is my elbows coming in to my sides and squeezing down, and I'm feeling my lats work and my shoulder blades squeezing together.

I am sure that my success as a bodybuilder is the result of a combination of good genetics and my training methods. I don't think I would be in the position I'm in now had I trained in a more conventional manner. However, I feel that I can always get better, and I continue to learn and develop new training methods. I love the feeling of effort and exertion—and this love has made it a little easier for me to endure the pain and frustration that often come with training and the pursuit of excellence.

I love all forms of movement, and enjoy trying out new sports. I always wanted to try karate; the combination of speed, power, skill, and self-control is fascinating to me, but I've never had the time it requires. I've been a national champion in track and field, and a national and world champion in powerlifting. I've now been a world champion bodybuilder.

I don't like to see wasted potential, so my goal is to be the best bodybuilder in the world!

Here I am in 1983, at the *Pumping Iron II* competition.

My fans always demand the Most Muscular pose. Here, I'm doing a version at the 1987 Ms. Olympia, where I placed third.

1
BODYBUILDING BASICS

Onstage at the 1987 IFBB Women's World Professional Bodybuilding Championships — from left to right: Diana Dennis, fourth place; Winston Ruberts; my husband, Steve, and I; Wayne DeMilia, IFBB vice-president; and Anja Langer, second place.

Bodybuilding is one of the toughest sports on earth. Not only do we train as hard and consistently as any other athlete, but we often do it with very small energy reserves due to a strict precontest diet. It takes an awesome degree of drive and self-discipline to push through a 1½- to 2-hour workout when you don't have any energy to expend. Any way you cut it, that type of training hurts.

As tough as bodybuilding is, it also provides its devotees with unique rewards. One of these is the satisfaction that comes with achieving excellence despite the difficulties along the way. I simply can't describe how good it feels to stand on the victory plinth, accepting a first-place trophy. It feels great, and you'll be after that feeling, too, once you've experienced it.

Improved appearance and health as well as higher energy levels are other obvious rewards you'll get by following the bodybuilding lifestyle. Most people these days admire a well-conditioned, muscular, and athletic-looking woman. "How can I get legs like yours?" is just one example of the types of questions women ask me over and over again. Most of these women would like to appear stronger and leaner. It feels terrific to look this good.

Even though it is anaerobic in nature, weight training provides the heart, lungs, and muscles with abundant aerobic conditioning. And the glow of general health exhibited by all bodybuilders is certain evidence that the inner workings are in tip-top order.

Additional strength and energy are also appealing by-products of the bodybuilding training and diet. If you are in shape, that heavy bag of groceries will feel like a feather, and you can literally dance all night long. I never feel low in energy, except for the final couple of weeks prior to a competition when all bodybuilders have problems keeping their energy up.

All of the foregoing rewards from the bodybuilding lifestyle are extrinsic—that is, readily perceived by yourself and those around you. But there are also intrinsic rewards that come from bodybuilding that are less readily visible. They include self-confidence, self-esteem, the ability to tackle and complete difficult tasks, the skill to set and achieve complex goals, the drive to excel at life, and grace in both winning and losing on the contest platform and in life in general.

Given all of these rewards derived from following the bodybuilding lifestyle, is there any doubt in your mind about wanting to be a bodybuilder? I have no doubts for myself—that's for sure!

Two-way neck machine.

MUSCLE HYPERTROPHY

Muscle hypertrophy is the increase in mass, strength, and tone of the skeletal muscles resulting from a work overload placed upon them. If this work overload is gradually and consistently increased, you will be able to make progressively greater increases in muscle hypertrophy over the years, until you have developed enough muscle mass and quality to win a major bodybuilding title.

Weight training used to be called progressive resistance exercise because the load placed on each skeletal muscle was progressively and systematically increased over a period of time. In bodybuilding circles, this technique for increasing resistance is called progression. The progression of the training load is the foundation of all methods of bodybuilding training.

To understand progression, you will need to learn a few simple terms, based upon the following model:

EXERCISE	SETS	REPS
Bench Presses	4	8–12
Incline Dumbbell Presses	3	8–12
Cross-Bench Dumbbell Pullovers	3	10–15

The first term is *exercise*. An exercise is each individual movement performed in a training program or workout—for example, Bench Presses, Incline Dumbbell Presses, and Cross-Bench Pullovers in the foregoing model. An exercise is often referred to as a movement.

A *set* is any distinct, individual grouping of *repetitions* (or counts) performed consecutively and separated by a *rest interval* before the next set begins. Set is a mathematics term that has

Bench Press — start/finish.

Bench Press—midpoint.

been co-opted for use in bodybuilding. Normally, a set consists of 5 to 20 repetitions (reps) in a bodybuilding scenario. Rest intervals normally last between 30 and 120 seconds.

When a *program* (also called a routine or training schedule, denoting either the written or performed list of exercises, sets, and reps) is written down, a range of reps is usually given for each exercise. The lower and upper number of each range is called the *lower guide number* and the *upper guide number*. In the line following Bench Presses in the foregoing model, 8 is the lower guide number and 12 the upper guide number for reps.

In normal bodybuilding progression, you will start out doing a set with a specific *poundage* (or *weight*) at the lower guide number. Then you will gradually increase repetitions for each succeeding workout until you reach the upper guide number. The next time you train, you will add 5 or 10 pounds to the barbell,

decrease the reps back to the lower guide number, and then begin the build-up process over again.

As a serious bodybuilder, you will be expected to repeat the build-up process just described almost *ad infinitum*—and, in doing so, you will develop a great deal of strength and muscle mass. It is an axiom in bodybuilding that the stronger you are for reps in a particular basic exercise, the larger will be the muscles used in that exercise. In other words, lift big to get big.

Assuming that you are doing one set of 8 to 12 reps in the Bench Press, your progression for 4 weeks might look like this:

	DAY 1	DAY 2	DAY 3
Week 1	100 × 8	100 × 9	100 × 10
Week 2	100 × 12	105 × 8	105 × 9
Week 3	105 × 9	105 × 10	105 × 11
Week 4	105 × 12	110 × 8	110 × 9

In most bodybuilding workouts, you will be expected to do multiple sets of each movement in your training program. Then you must get each of the required sets up to the upper guide number before increasing resistance. The following is an example of this more complex form of progression for Incline Barbell Presses, involving 4 sets of 6 to 10 repetitions:

	DAY 1	DAY 2	DAY 3
Week 1	80 × 8	80 × 10	80 × 11
	80 × 8	80 × 9	80 × 10
	80 × 8	80 × 8	80 × 9
	80 × 8	80 × 8	80 × 9
Week 2	80 × 12	80 × 12	80 × 12
	80 × 11	80 × 12	80 × 12
	80 × 10	80 × 11	80 × 12
	80 × 9	80 × 10	80 × 10
Week 3	80 × 12	80 × 12	85 × 8
	80 × 12	80 × 12	85 × 8
	80 × 12	80 × 12	85 × 8
	80 × 11	80 × 12	85 × 7
Week 4	85 × 9	85 × 10	85 × 11
	85 × 8	85 × 9	85 × 10
	85 × 8	85 × 9	85 × 9
	85 × 8	85 × 8	85 × 8

While you should constantly push as hard as possible to add a minimum of one new repetition during each succeeding workout, on some days you won't be able to do so. This is due to a number of factors—among them lack of sleep, poor diet, and the natural up-and-down energy fluctuations each body undergoes. When these days occur, be sure to add extra reps during your next workout to make up for any lost ground.

One-arm dumbbell Preacher Curls.

Steve and I.

PHYSICAL EXAMS

The following advice is for women who have not been actively working out with weights. If you are over 35 years of age or have been sedentary for at least 2 years, you should make an appointment with a physician and have a physical examination. If you have been sedentary for a longer period of time or are over 40 years of age, that examination should include a stress test electrocardiogram.

From a physical exam, a physician can determine whether you are fit and healthy enough to survive the rigors of bodybuilding training. If the doctor suggests going lighter or less intensively than I do, by all means, follow his advice.

WHERE TO WORK OUT

There are many good places to train as a bodybuilder. The best is a commercial gym, like the one Steve and I own in Syosset, New York, or like those in the large chain of hardcore bodybuilding emporiums established across the United States by Gold's Gym or the World Gym. Most commercial gyms will allow you try out the facilities with an orientation workout, after which you can decide if you want to train there.

Your decision to join a particular gym should be based on the variety of equipment it offers, the hours it's open, and what you perceive to be the members' general level of enthusiasm. You also might want to consider whether the gym offers you access to high-level bodybuilders who can give you personal advice.

You probably won't feel too comfortable at the chromed-up health spas. It's likely that the people in the administration at these money-making operations will discourage you from training very hard or heavy, since they probably feel you will scare off some potential members who might make them even more money. Most health spas tend not to have heavy enough equipment for a serious bodybuilder anyway.

On the other hand, some YMCAs have excellent heavy weight rooms, as do many colleges and universities. In evaluating both Y and school gyms, use the same criteria suggested for commercial gyms.

If a good gym is not available in your area, you can always set up a good home gym in your garage or basement. All it takes is an investment of about $500 and a little innovation. With a home gym, you won't have the camaraderie that comes with training at a commercial gym, but you'll have access to it 24 hours a day, something that can't be said for many commercial establishments.

If you do choose to work out in a home gym, think about pooling equipment with other bodybuilders in your neighborhood. This way, you'll have access to a wider range of equipment, and perhaps also meet a dependable training partner who can offer you encouragement and be a good spotter when the going gets heavy in your workouts. (For more about training partners, turn to pages 26 and 28.)

EXERCISE POUNDAGES

At the end of this chapter, you will find a couple of workouts. The first one is for women who haven't had much experience with bodybuilding training, the second for women one step up from the beginning level. If you've had some experience in a gym, you'll already have a pretty good idea about how strong you are and how much weight you can safely use in each exercise. But if you don't have much experience, it would be a good idea to take my suggestions for starting poundages on every movement.

In the Beginning-Level Workout, I have listed suggested starting weights based on a percentage of your body weight. Merely multiply the given percentage by your body weight in pounds, and then round down to the nearest 5-pound increment, and you'll be in business. But keep in mind that everyone has different strength levels. If the weight is so heavy that you can't complete 10 reps comfortably, reduce it by a few pounds. Or, if you can easily complete 12 reps, add a little weight the next time you work out.

REST INTERVALS

When bodybuilding, you should be conscious of the length of rest intervals between sets. Gener-

Hanging Leg Raises — start.

ally, you should rest enough between sets to recover sufficient energy and strength to do justice to your next set. Base the length of time you rest according to the mass of the body parts you're using; the larger parts, such as your overall legs and back, require more rest between sets than the smaller ones, like your biceps and triceps. But you should avoid resting more than 2 minutes between even the heaviest sets of leg and back work, since resting more than this would allow your body to cool down between sets, leaving you more open to injury.

As discussed earlier in this chapter, you can increase training load by adding repetitions to your sets or weight to a barbell; but you can also increase training intensity by reducing the length of rest intervals between sets. This method is used almost exclusively over the last few weeks prior to a competition. It is called quality training, and will be discussed in detail in Chapter 7.

CORRECT FORM

Use of strict form, sometimes called biomechanics, is important for two reasons: It allows you to transfer the maximum possible amount of stress to the working muscles during each repetition, rather than allowing extraneous muscle groups to take over some of the work—and it helps prevent injuries.

Proper form starts with a commitment to moving *only* those parts of the body called for in the movement. It continues with keeping this commitment in mind as you consistently carry out full repetitions, moving each muscle from a position of full extension to one of full contraction and back again to full extension.

Correct form does not involve kicking with your knees, hunching your torso forward or backward, doing short movements, or otherwise cheating yourself out of the exercise you should be getting when you do a set.

There *is* a time, however, when cheating is essential in a power-bodybuilding training session. Judicious use of cheating allows you to push your muscles harder than is possible when training in strict form. If you start a set with strict biomechanics and continue it to the point

Hanging Leg Raises — finish.

of momentary muscular failure—say, after at least 5 or 6 strict reps—you can then cheat a little to push your muscles to continue working past the normal failure point. That, in turn, will induce a larger amount of muscle hypertrophy in a shorter-than-normal period of time.

BREATHING PATTERNS

Oxygen is not only necessary to keep you alive, but also to fuel your muscle contractions. Although breathing comes naturally, it must be regimented when you are training with weights to keep you from growing faint.

There are two schools of thought when it comes to breathing during each repetition:

- Inhale as you lower the weight, and exhale as you push it back up to the starting point of the movement.
- Exhale as you lower the weight, and inhale as you push it back up to the starting point.

I recommend the first way. Once you practice it for a week or so, you'll find that breathing in such a manner will become so automatic that you won't have to think about it.

WORKOUT WEAR

Climate and temperature dictate what you should wear for a workout. In temperate areas or when the temperature is warm, you may only need to wear shorts and a T-shirt (plus underwear and shoes). But when the weather is colder, you will need to dress more warmly to keep from getting chilled and incurring an injury.

Generally, you should wear several thin layers of clothing rather than one or two thick layers, shedding a layer or two as you get thoroughly warmed up. For example, you might wear tights and one or two pairs of warm-up pants to cover your lower body, and several T-shirts and/or track-suit tops over your upper body.

All bodybuilders should wear shoes with built-in arch supports. Shoes will protect your feet from injury should you drop a loose barbell plate on them, and the arch supports will prevent the arches of your feet from getting compression injuries caused by supporting a heavy weight in a basic movement. It's also a good idea to wear shoes with treads, which will securely grip a calf block when you're doing exercises for the posterior muscles of the lower leg.

Running shoes answer all of the foregoing requirements, and can be bought almost everywhere, even by mail-order through ads in sports magazines. Cost varies widely, from about $30 to more than $100 per pair. For about $50, you can purchase a pair that will probably last a couple of years.

CHANGING ROUTINES

When you follow one routine for too long a period of time, your mind and body will become so accustomed to it that you will begin to make slower and slower gains in muscle hypertrophy from your workouts. Therefore, it's necessary to change to a new training schedule every 4 to 6 weeks as a means of maintaining a good rate of muscle-mass gains.

At the end of this chapter are two suggested routines. If you start out doing the Beginning-Level Workout, stay on it for 6 weeks; then switch to the Intermediate-Level Workout. After 6 weeks on that program, you should be sufficiently well conditioned to move on to a normal off-season bodybuilding training regimen.

Although it's uncommon, there are some people who don't need to change routines so often. If you don't grow bored and are continuing to make good gains, "don't fix something that isn't broken."

TRAINING PARTNERS

Most top bodybuilders use training partners. A workout partner is particularly useful for spotting you and for giving you forced reps (if you use the technique to push a set past the normal failure point, which I usually don't). Prior to a show, a training partner can also help you keep the pace of your workout up, even when you are very low on energy due to your peaking diet. And it's much more difficult to miss a workout when you know your partner is at the gym waiting for you to show up.

Most top bodybuilders use training partners.

When choosing a training partner, first look for someone who has a level of workout enthusiasm at least as high as your own. While high-level competitors usually have a great deal of training drive, you'll find other lower-level bodybuilders with lots of enthusiasm, as well. However, there's no reason why you should pull someone with less incentive through his or her workout; that would undoubtedly hold you back.

It's also a good idea to choose someone at or near your strength levels. When using an adjustable Olympic barbell, for instance, you won't have to change weights so often if you train with a bodybuilder who's as strong as you are. Obviously, strength levels will vary with certain body parts—particularly if you are training with a male partner—but try to work out with a partner who is basically at your own level.

Incidentally, strength levels *do* vary between the sexes. Generally, a 150-pound woman will be weaker than a 150-pound man, although I certainly was much stronger than most men my weight—even those who train—when powerlifting competitively. In comparison to men, women tend to be stronger in the legs and weaker in the upper body. However, I still think it's beneficial to train with someone of the opposite sex. Men can push women to use heavier poundages; and since women have better endurance and resistance to fatigue-oriented pain, they can thus push their male partners to train harder and longer.

Finally, it's always wise to choose a training partner who has the same basic goals as you do. Say, if you are training hard for a competition with a partner who is only interested in overall body conditioning, you would probably be out of sync. It would be much better to train with someone who is also aiming at competition. You may be shooting for competitions on different dates, but that would actually be advantageous since it's better to have a least one workout partner at full strength, rather than depleted as a result of a precontest diet.

Although a minority of top bodybuilders train on their own, this is still a valid approach to take. Normally, solitary trainers tend to be individualists and self-starters who have no trouble motivating themselves to train consistently hard. They also usually take a highly individualistic and instinctive approach to their workouts, listening to their bodies closely and adjusting each daily workout to precisely suit their present goals and needs.

WARM-UPS

Bodybuilders who fail to warm up properly before every workout are cutting their careers short. Failure to warm up correctly is an open invitation to injury. If you don't warm up, you're bound to get either a serious sprain, strain, or muscle connective-tissue rupture—or, even more likely, long-term microtraumas that ultimately can lead to disabling sore joints.

In addition to preventing injury, warming up makes it possible to use more weight in each exercise than if you started out cold, and it also helps tune up motor coordination skills.

A proper warm-up should consist of aerobic work, stretching, and calisthenics exercises, followed by light weight work. It should last between 10 and 15 minutes, and should leave you feeling warm, with accelerated pulse and respiration rates. If you are perspiring lightly, that can be a sign that you're probably ready for a good, heavy weight workout.

Studies have shown that stretching a cold muscle or joint can cause microinjuries; so, start out your warm-up by either riding a stationary bike or jogging in place for 3 or 4 minutes. Only then should you stretch out each joint and muscle group, a process that can take up to 5 minutes. Your final nonweight warm-up process involves doing Push-Ups and other calisthenics exercises for several minutes. Be sure to do exercises that affect each part of your body.

For the light weight part of your warm-up, it's best to do high-rep sets of basic movements for each muscle group, which can be part of the first exercise for a particular body part. A good example would be bench presses for your chest, in which you do 2 or 3 high-repetition (20 to 25 reps) sets with increasingly heavier poundages, until you arrive at your first building-weight set. This way, you'll be thoroughly warmed up and

Cooling off after winning world championships (1987).

Deadlifts — start.

Deadlifts — finish. (Note the use of straps for grips.)

When using maximum weights in power exercises, you will often have to use straps to reinforce your grip on the bar. Start by slipping your hand through the loop on the strap, and then begin to wind the strap around the bar, as shown.

Pull the end of the strap tight to pull your wrist down towards the bar.

Grasp the bar with your thumb and the palm of your hand over the strap. As long as you don't relax your grip, the strap will stay tight around the bar. To loosen your grip, merely open your hand and pull the strap free.

ready to tackle even the heaviest weights without fear of injury.

SUGGESTED ROUTINES

Here are two suggested workouts, which you can use to condition your body for true hardcore bodybuilding sessions. The first one can be used for about 6 weeks, three times per week—the second for 6 to 8 weeks, four times a week.

Beginning-Level Workout

MONDAY, WEDNESDAY, AND FRIDAY

EXERCISE	SETS	REPS	BODY WT.
Incline Sit-Ups	2–3	15–20	—
Angled Leg Presses	3	10–15	75%
Deadlifts	3	6–10	75%
Barbell Bent Rows	3	8–12	50%
Bench Presses	3	6–10	50%
Dumbbell Side Laterals	2	8–12	5% (each)
Barbell Curls	2	8–12	25%
Pulley Push-Downs	2	8–12	15%
Standing Calf Raises	3	15–20	60%

Intermediate-Level Workout

MONDAY AND THURSDAY

EXERCISE	SETS	REPS
Hanging-Leg Raises	3	10–15
Bench Presses	4	6–10
Incline Dumbbell Presses	3	6–10
Presses Behind Neck	3	6–10
Barbell Upright Rows	3	8–12
Dumbbell Side Laterals	2	8–12
Chins	4	8–12
Seated Pulley Rows	3	8–12

TUESDAY AND FRIDAY

EXERCISE	SETS	REPS
Crunches	3	20–30
Squats	4	8–15
Leg Extensions	3	10–15
Leg Curls	3	10–15
Deadlifts	4	6–10
Close-Grip Bench Presses	3	8–12
Pulley Push-Downs	2	8–12
Standing Barbell Curls	3	8–12
One-Arm Dumbbell Preacher Curls	4	8–12
Donkey Calf Raises	4	15–20

Standing Barbell Curls.

Close-Grip Bench Press — start/finish.

Close-Grip Bench Press — midpoint.

Seated Calf Raises — start.

Seated Calf Raises — finish.

Crunch (feet-over-bench version) — start.

Crunch (feet-over-bench version) — finish.

You will find another more strenuous bodybuilding routine in the next chapter. You can use this routine—with occasional revision—during off-season cycles for just about as long as you are involved in bodybuilding. Good luck with your workouts!

Donkey Calf Raises

2
POWER-BODYBUILDING TRAINING

Parallel Bar Dips — start/finish.

Heavy weights build big muscles—this applies to women as well as to men. The heavier the weight you use in a building set of reps, the larger and more dense your muscles.

This chapter is about the basics of building muscle through power training the Bev Francis way. Power bodybuilding is appropriate for both beginners and intermediates seeking to develop sufficient muscle mass to enter competition. It is also appropriate for contest-level bodybuilders when training to bring up a weak body part and increase general muscle mass during an off-season cycle.

Handling heavy weights in somewhat looser-than-normal form for selected basic movements is the basis behind power-body-building training. Good form is very important for bodybuilders, but not all of the time. Occasionally during the off-season, I cheat to make a set harder on my muscles. Although I loosen up my form mainly on the basics, I also do it on some isolation exercises, such as Dumbbell Side Laterals.

However, prior to a competition—when I'm aiming primarily for refinement—power-bodybuilding training for additional mass isn't appropriate. It's a good idea to do some heavy sets of one basic exercise per muscle group once or twice a week before a show because that helps maintain muscle mass as you diet down to competition body-fat levels, but pure power training before a contest is unproductive and can lead to injuries.

When deciding whether or not to throw in a power day, I also take into consideration my relative energy level. I avoid handling a lot of weight when I'm feeling tired because it's much easier to get injured when you're too fatigued to maintain a good mind-muscle connection during every set. Deficient general health (anything less than 100 percent) usually causes some fatigue. So, even if I'm in the middle of a pre-planned power-training cycle, I might either go lighter or do more isolation exercises when my energy level is not up where it should be. The next workout I'm usually back up to par and can go heavy again. Lethargy generally doesn't last more than a day or two, unless you have a significant underlying health problem.

The rep range for solely building strength is much lower than for developing optimum amounts of muscle mass. Low-repetition training builds tendon and connective-tissue strength as well as muscle-contractile ability but little appreciable muscle tissue. Since there is a greater risk of injury when doing singles, doubles, or triples, most top powerlifters do sets of about 5 to 8 repetitions when attempting to increase brute strength. That repetition range is also conducive to building muscle mass, as evidenced by some of the incredibly massive physiques displayed on international powerlifting platforms.

In my own case, I did sets of 8 to 10 reps most of the time when I was powerlifting, with only infrequent low-repetition sets to test my strength levels in each power lift as a competition approached. As a consequence of using this repetition range, I gained so much muscle mass that I was eventually encouraged to enter a pro-bodybuilding competition. My considered opinion is that huge muscle mass is developed by foundation work with reps in the range of 8 to 10, rather than by doing heavy, low-rep workouts.

Between mass-building and muscle-refining cycles, my repetitions don't really change that much. They usually are in the 8-to-15 range year-round. What changes is the form—looser when power-training, ultrastrict when peaking for competition—and the length of the rest intervals between sets. Because I train faster and faster on a calorie-restricted diet as I near a competition, at that time my exercise poundages inevitably drop markedly below those I use off-season.

In the suggested Power-Bodybuilding Routine at the end of this chapter, most of the heavy sets are done in a half-pyramid fashion, in which you increase the weights and reduce the reps each succeeding set. Using descending sets will also do the job, since that's a great way to handle heavy poundages while doing a lot of reps each set. (If you're unfamiliar with the descending-sets technique, you will find a detailed explanation of it in Chapter 6.)

Parallel Bar Dips — midpoint.

Cable Bent-Over Laterals — start.

Cable Bent-Over Laterals — finish.

Barbell Bent-Over Rows — midpoint.

One technique I don't use much is forced reps during a power cycle. One reason is that back home in Australia when I was training for track and field and powerlifting, I was frequently the only person in the weight room. Obviously, you can't do forced reps without at least one training partner, so the technique didn't become part of my training program.

I also hate to be still moving on a near-maximum-poundage rep and have someone actually lift the weight up for me, which usually happens when someone gives me forced reps. On the rare sets when I continue past failure with a forced rep or two, I prefer to have my partner push down on the bar for the first few reps—causing me to make a maximum effort for almost every repetition—and then help me minimally with a forced rep or two when my muscles are almost fully exhausted. In other words, every repetition of my set is manually adjusted to match my strength level from one rep to the next. This sort of training requires a partner who knows you very well. That is why my husband, Steve, is my only training partner.

In my training seminars, a lot of women ask me, "What's the point of lifting heavy weights?"

Barbell Bent-Over Rows — near finish.

Seated Pulley Rows (wear gloves to protect hands) — start.

The answer is simple—the stronger you are on a building set of 10 reps, the larger your muscles. I said this at the beginning of the chapter, but it merits emphasis. If you can squat with 400 pounds for 3 reps, then a building set with 330 will actually feel light by comparison. And these building sets in turn will increase your strength threshold, further advancing the power- and mass-building process.

I believe that women need power cycles even more than men. Women naturally tend to feel the weight rather than attack it, and attacking the weight is the style in which heavy poundages are lifted in basic exercises. It's im-

Seated Pulley Rows — finish.

Dumbbell Side Laterals — start.

portant for women bodybuilders to learn this aggressive approach to a heavy set mainly because it builds self-confidence. Even if you're dealing with a huge poundage, you know that you will be able to move the bar up to the finish point of the basic movement. You may have to move it quite slowly if it's very close to your limit, but you will still be able to do it.

The foregoing concept is actually the reverse of my own learning process. Since I trained for power long before bodybuilding, I knew how to aggressively lift a weight. Powerlifters are lifters and bodybuilders are feelers, so when I made the switch I had to learn to feel my muscles contracting against the weight. Now I'm so intently focused on the feeling in my working muscles that I can barely sense the weight in my hands as I do an exercise. That's the approach I eventually had to master to bring out all the fine muscle detail necessary to win a pro-bodybuilding title.

Women bodybuilding competitors have to be tigers in the gym, not meek little mice. You have to train hard, heavy, and fast to build the ideal combination of muscle mass and detail. But once you learn to be more aggressive with the heavier weights—once you become a power bodybuilder—you'll find that your training sessions can be a fantastic outlet for pent-up emotional energy.

Training is only part of the picture when you're going specifically for power and muscle mass; proper recovery is also important. If you fail to recover between your heavy workouts, you won't make much progress. Enough sleep and rest are essential for between-workouts recovery. Constantly monitor yourself for symptoms of overtraining—such as fatigue, lethargy, persistent soreness, and lack of enthusiasm for workouts—and then take steps to improve deficient recovery ability.

Correct nutrition when you're power mass-building is also essential. You'll find a comprehensive discussion of the topic in Chapter 4.

The final key to progress when you are power-bodybuilding is maintaining a positive attitude. You *will* reach your goals. Nothing can stop you as long as your training, diet, and

Dumbbell Side Laterals — finish.

recovery are in order. So, hammer it—you'll be great!

Note: This routine can be used by men as well as by women, set for set and rep for rep. It's just that male bodybuilders will be proportionately stronger than women.

Power-Bodybuilding Routine

MONDAY AND THURSDAY

EXERCISE	SETS	REPS
Bench Press (warm-up)	2–3	15–20
	5	10–6*
Incline Dumbbell Presses	4–5	10–6*
Parallel Bar Dips (weighted)	4–5	8–12
Behind Neck Presses (warm-up)	1–2	15–20
	5	10–6*
Dumbbell Side Laterals	3–4	8–12
Cable Bent Laterals	3–4	8–12
Standing Barbell Curls	3–4	10–6*
One-Arm Dumbbell Preacher Curls	3–4	8–12
Close-Grip Bench Presses	3–4	10–6*
Pulley Push-Downs	3–4	8–12

TUESDAY AND FRIDAY

EXERCISE	SETS	REPS
Squats (warm-up)	2–3	15–20
	6	12–6*
Leg Presses (45°)	5	10–6*
Leg Extensions	5	8–12
Lying Leg Curls	4	8–12
Standing Leg Curls	3	8–12
Front Chins, or . . .	3	maximum
Front Lat Pull-Downs	3	10–6*
Barbell Bent Rows, or . . .	3	10–6*
Machine Rows	3	10–6*
Seated Low-Pulley Rows	3	10–6*
Deadlifts, or . . .	3	10–6*
Hyperextensions (no added weight)	3	15–20
Machine Donkey Calf Raises, or . . .	5	8–25**
Standing Calf Raises	5	8–25**
Seated Calf Raises	4	8–25**
Hanging-Leg Raises	3–5	15–20
Crunches (vary type)	3–5	20–30

*Pyramid weight and reps
**Vary reps (heavy, medium, light) on calf movements from one workout to the next, and avoid the same rep range on both calf exercises in a workout.

Presses Behind Neck (on Smith machine) — start.

Presses Behind Neck — finish.

3
ADVANCED BODYBUILDING PRINCIPLES

The topic of bodybuilding potential pervades the sport. Does she have the skeletal structure to become a national champion? Does she have any genetic weak points? Is she intelligent enough to master the more scientific aspects of bodybuilding? And the list goes on. . . .

When I host a training seminar, probably the most frequently asked question is, "Do I have the potential to be a winner?".

Physical and mental potential for bodybuilding is difficult to determine on your own. Evaluating your potential usually takes the experienced eye of a coach, gym owner, or competitor. And many of the factors that determine bodybuilding potential can't be assessed until an athlete has trained consistently for a year or two.

The first question to ask yourself is whether you are sufficiently motivated to succeed in the sport. Are you willing to endure the deprivations and self-sacrifices that are necessarily part of successful competitive bodybuilding? If you don't have a lot of motivation, whatever innate potential you actually possess will go sadly to waste.

Before you even begin regular workouts, the following eight factors in combination are good indications of outstanding bodybuilding potential:

- relatively broad shoulders in relation to your waist and hips;
- a narrow waist;
- a relatively narrow hip structure;
- limbs that are proportionate in length to your torso physiognomy;
- small joints (wrists, knees, ankles);
- a naturally high degree of muscle mass;
- a relatively low percentage of body fat; and
- a high degree of intelligence.

After you have put in about a year of consistent training and have developed some degree of muscle mass, the following three factors can be added to the above list:

Reverse Curls (top position).

• You have no completely unresponsive body parts (everyone has lagging muscle groups from time to time, but totally underdeveloped body parts will condemn you to bodybuilding mediocrity).
• You are gaining general muscle mass quickly enough to keep your interest level in training at a high peak.
• You have shown a capacity to understand and master the more scientific aspects of the bodybuilding process.

Some people might question my inclusion of intelligence and ability to understand the technical aspects of the sport in my lists, but bodybuilding has become a highly technical and scientific activity and the day is long past when an unintelligent woman with superior physical potential can win the bigger titles just on physical talent alone.

Undoubtedly, very few readers will possess all of the foregoing factors indicating high bodybuilding potential. Indeed, very few women will have even nine or 10. However, it's important to realize that there are great bodybuilding champions currently competing with an admittedly dismal potential for the sport. Bodybuilding potential should not be considered a *limiting* factor, but rather an *enabling* one. It's just easier and faster for those with superior natural talent to reach the top, but all bodybuilders can achieve an outstanding degree of muscular development if they are willing to put in the effort, stay consistently dedicated to making improvement, and stick it out for a sufficiently long period of time.

One thing that's so great about bodybuilding is that you get results in direct proportion to the amount of work and dietary dedication you put into the sport. So, if you don't have the best bodybuilding potential, don't use it as an excuse for not making good gains. Work hard, and you'll eventually build a great physique.

MUSCLE PRIORITY

All bodybuilders have individual muscle complexes that improve at varying rates of speed. Some body parts seem to explode in development as a consequence of almost no training intensity, whereas others respond very slowly, if at all. Your ability to balance your physical proportions by holding back responsive groups and bringing up stubborn areas will make or break you as a bodybuilding competitor.

Balanced physical proportions become increasingly more important as you rise from level to level in the sport. At my own professional level of competition, balanced proportions are mandatory. So, you should make a special effort to identify weak points and train them with maximum intensity via the muscle-priority technique until they are up to par with the rest of your physique.

Sometimes one or two muscle groups will prove to be consistently weak; also, weak parts will often occur when the areas have been neglected in a training program. The important point, however, is the necessity of identifying these weak areas—either personally by way of looking at your appearance in the mirror or in physique photos, or with the assistance of a coach, trainer, or gym owner.

Judges can also be an important source of evaluation if you approach them politely after a show you've entered. Ask them: "What area or areas should I bring up in order to place higher next time?" As long as you're sincere and polite, the judges will give you honest—and valuable—evaluations of your weak points.

A lagging body part must be priority-trained. This means working a weak area first each training session, when you have the most physical and mental energy to expend on all-out training to improve that area. Towards the end of a workout, you should be too fatigued to put a 100 percent effort into working a stubborn muscle complex.

It is not a good idea, however, to use priority training with the upper-arm muscles. If you train your biceps or triceps prior to your torso workout, your arm muscles will be weaker than normal, and this in turn will inhibit your ability to get in a good chest, back, or shoulder workout. If your biceps or triceps are weak, you should strongly consider training your arms in a

Training with maximum intensity.

Squat — midpoint (one-quarter Squat).

Squat — midpoint (half Squat).

Squat — finish.

workout separate from that for the rest of your physique.

Actually, *any* exceptionally weak area should be trained by itself, particularly if it's a comparatively large muscle complex, like the legs or back. This will allow you to expend a great deal of energy in a relatively short workout, which means that your energy levels will be high throughout the entire session. Let me give you an example of how this works.

Assuming that your thigh muscles (quadriceps and/or hamstrings) are badly lagging behind the rest of your physique, here is a sample split routine that will allow you to place maximum priority on your quads and thigh biceps:

   Monday and Thursday: chest, back, delts, upper arms, forearms, calves

   Tuesday and Friday: quads (lots of Squats!), hamstrings, abdominals

Spending a few months on this type of split routine will substantially improve your upper legs.

INCREASING TRAINING INTENSITY

For advanced bodybuilders, increases in training intensity come primarily from using cheating and/or forced reps. (They also use a more complex intensification technique called descending sets, which is discussed in Chapter 6.)

As I've mentioned, I prefer cheating reps—using looser form and a bit of extraneous body motion—over forced reps when increasing my own intensity levels. Don't get the idea that I recommend one technique over the other, however. My choice is mainly a consequence of my early training environment and lack of workout partners to spot me for forced reps.

However, I should caution you against using too much of a cheat on a rep, or cheating too early in a set. For optimum workout intensity, begin your set in strict fashion and get at least 5 or 6 reps in before you begin cheating. When you do begin to cheat, give the bar just enough momentum to allow your working muscles to complete the rep. Never do a repetition completely with a cheat because that would be a waste of effort.

With their working muscles becoming progressively more fatigued very quickly, some bodybuilders find it difficult to give the right amount of momentum to the bar for a perfect cheating rep. These bodybuilders either cheat too much and the bar flies up, or they cheat too little and it doesn't go up at all. Thus, for them, forced reps would be a better alternative.

In forced reps, a training partner stands over you and pulls up on the bar or machine lever just enough each time to allow you to finish the rep under your own power. This might mean pulling up with 5 pounds of effort, or 50, depending on how many forced reps you have completed and how close your muscles are to total fatigue breakdown. In actuality, more than 2 or 3 forced reps at the end of an otherwise strict set will be excessive because your muscles will simply be too fatigued to contract efficiently.

Forced reps take some real teamwork, as well as sensitivity on the part of your training partner, so that he or she doesn't pull up on the

bar before you actually fail a rep, or pull up with more force than is necessary. For this reason, it's best to use the same training partner most of the time when you're doing forced repetitions.

INJURIES

Bodybuilders often suffer injuries due to inattention to proper warm-up procedures, failure to maintain strict exercise form with maximum poundages, or a deficiency in general health. Sometimes, however, injuries are simply a result of training consistently at the upper edge of maximum training intensity.

I've had my share of injuries over the years, but primarily when I was involved in track and field and powerlifting. The injuries I've suffered in bodybuilding training have been minor in comparison. But this isn't to say that serious injuries never occur in bodybuilding, because they do.

Earlier, I said that competitive success is dependent on your ability to bring weak muscle groups up to par with the rest of your physique. In a very real sense, it also depends on your ability to avoid injuries, train around what chronic injuries you might have from other sports, and recover quickly from bodybuilding-related injuries. Long-lasting injuries can dramatically retard the speed with which you make gains in muscle mass and achieve your goals.

If you get a major injury—a broken bone, dislocated joint, torn muscle, ruptured tendon, or any other serious tissue disruption—you should immediately see your physician. If you don't have an orthopedist, a general practitioner might suffice. But if the injury is serious enough, the general practitioner will probably refer you to an orthopedist, who may perform surgery to correct the injury. Some of my track and powerlifting injuries have required surgery.

On the other hand, you can usually treat minor injuries—strains and sprains—yourself at home in a speedy and efficient manner. The technique for curing a minor injury is called *RICE*, which stands for rest, ice, compression, and elevation. Rest is an obvious requisite for healing, and ice, compression, and elevation decrease the swelling at the injury site. The more swelling you have, the slower the injury will heal.

Minor injuries should be immediately iced, either by rubbing ice directly on the injury site or by holding a plastic bag of ice cubes wrapped in a moist towel over the injured area. For the first couple of hours, you should apply the ice for about 5 minutes (or however long your skin can stand the cold), take a break for 10 to 15 minutes, and then apply the ice again. For the next 24 hours, the ice should be applied for 5 to 10 minutes every waking hour.

To achieve compression, firmly wrap an elastic gauze bandage over the area. But you need to periodically loosen the gauze for a few minutes to permit normal blood flow, particularly if you've wrapped it completely around an arm or leg.

Elevation simply allows fluids to move naturally out of the injured area.

In combination, rest, ice, compression, and elevation can be quite effective in limiting swelling at the injury site. But you have to use each diligently and consistently, or you'll limit the technique's effectiveness.

You can begin to stretch the affected muscle or joint 4 or 5 days after the injury. But go lightly, and be sure to ease up if you feel any injury-related pain. After about a week, you can begin light weight training following your stretching session, again easing up at the first hint of pain.

With patience and persistence, you should be back to a full training load and intensity level 3 or 4 weeks after a minor injury. Sometimes, you will be able to resume training even more quickly, but don't push too hard or too fast because you might reinjure yourself. Reinjuries take much longer to heal, and they can set back your progress significantly.

Of course, you should feel good about healing an injury and getting back up to a high level of training intensity, but your primary objective should be avoiding injuries in the first place. The best way to do this is by getting in a complete warm-up prior to each training session, staying warmed up throughout your entire workout, and maintaining good strict form when you're using maximum weights.

Crunch — free-style variation.

Proper warm-ups and optimum biomechanics will also prevent the long accumulation of microtraumas, which eventually build up to real injuries. If you want to limit long-term microtrauma, keep your reps up to at least 5 or 6 per set.

Bodybuilders with chronic injuries—particularly to the lower back—become experts at training around their injuries. When you have a sore lower back, for example, you can do most of your upper-body work while lying on a flat or inclined exercise bench. And you can do leg exercises—such as leg presses, leg extensions, and leg curls—that don't place stress on your lower back.

With experience, you can learn to train around any type of chronic injury—to your shoulders, elbows, wrists, knees, ankles, and so forth. This merely involves trying various exercises that affect the injured area, determining which ones aggravate the injury, and then avoiding those movements. At one time or another, almost all bodybuilders face the prospect of training around an injury; it's an integral part of bodybuilding and a skill that is important to acquire.

REST AND RECOVERY

Rest and recovery are essential requirements for muscle growth in bodybuilding. Unless you rest enough between workouts to permit complete recovery of the muscles and supporting systems (such as the cardiorespiratory system), muscle growth cannot occur. This means that you must understand the recovery cycle thoroughly, and work within its limits.

Your recovery system can be compared to your household budget. You put money (rest) into the system, and you pay it out (the way you expend energy in a workout) to the plumber, the carpet cleaner, the grocer, and so forth. But the important issue here is that you can't spend more money than you have allowed yourself in your budget. If you do, you go broke. The recovery cycle is very much the same. You put X amount of energy into the system by resting, eating correctly, avoiding nervous energy leaks, and getting sufficient sleep each night. You expend Y amount of energy in your workouts, both with weights and aerobically. As long as you don't allow Y to become chronically greater than X, you won't go energy broke.

Going energy broke in bodybuilding is basically overtraining—and overtraining will be one of your biggest obstacles as you climb up the competitive ladder. But if you understand what causes overtraining, you will be able to avoid it.

Overtraining almost always occurs when you train too long in the gym or on your exercise bike, rather than when you train too hard. Therefore, you should limit the duration of your workouts, rather than the intensity. Train hard and do relatively short workouts.

When you do too many total sets for each muscle group, you invariably build up so much residual fatigue that you eventually slip over the edge into an overtrained state. But how many sets are too many? The answer to that question depends primarily on how long you've been working out and, consequently, how efficient your recovery system has become.

The following are suggested maximum levels of total sets for each body part at various experience levels:

	BEGINNER	INTERMEDIATE
Legs	5–6	6–8
Back	5–6	6–8
Chest	5–6	6–8
Delts	4–5	5–7
Biceps	3–4	4–5
Triceps	3–4	4–5
Forearms	3–4	4–5
Calves	3–4	5–6
Abs	2–3	4–5

	ADVANCED	COMPETITIVE (OFF-SEASON)
Legs	8–10	12–15
Back	8–10	12–15
Chest	8–10	12–15
Delts	7–9	10–12
Biceps	6–8	8–10
Triceps	6–8	8–10
Forearms	6–8	8–10
Calves	7–9	10–12
Abs	6–7	8–10

Leg Extension.

Incidentally, you probably won't need to do direct neck work since that area tends to be affected by exercises for surrounding areas, such as the upper chest, shoulders, and upper back.

The foregoing list of total-set thresholds should be taken as a *suggestion* only. Obviously, every body is different and recovery ability varies from one bodybuilder to the next. It's best to experiment for several months to determine more exact thresholds for your own unique body.

Excessive aerobics can also lead to an overtrained state. I've seen this happen with a lot of competitors as they peak for a show. Panic causes some bodybuilders to radically increase the length of their aerobics sessions each day, which retards the recovery cycle, and they end up overtrained—looking flat and smooth onstage at their competition. So, be a bit conservative in your aerobic training when you are in a peaking cycle. Increase it *very* slowly.

How can you tell if you are overtrained? It's likely if you have one or more of the following symptoms:

- lack of enthusiasm for workouts,
- persistent fatigue,
- inability to sleep/difficulty in waking up,
- persistently sore joints and/or muscles,
- flu or other infections,
- deterioration of motor coordination,
- elevation of morning pulse rate, and
- elevation of morning blood pressure.

The last two factors can be easily determined if you take your pulse and/or blood pressure each morning and keep a record in your training diary. Pulse rate is particularly easy to note each day. A spike upwards in either pulse or blood pressure, and you are undoubtedly overtrained.

If you have overtrained, take a short layoff from the gym. The length of your layoff can vary from a few days to several weeks, depending on how severely overtrained you have become. Usually, you can accurately tell when you should get back to the gym when you have regained your enthusiasm for your workouts.

After your layoff, be sure that you both shorten and intensify your workouts. A reduction of 20 percent in total sets should do the trick. Remember, it's the length of your workout rather than it's level of intensity that will drive you into an overtrained condition.

MACHINES VERSUS FREE WEIGHTS

There has been a proliferation in brands of resistance-training machines in recent years, and with it has come a controversy of sorts: Which is better, free weights or machines? Actually, the answer is not particularly clear-cut because there are advantages and disadvantages to both types of apparatus.

Machines, in general, provide greater safety when you are training with weights because they operate along mechanical arcs from which they can't deviate. If you fail a rep, you simply need to return to the bottom position of the movement, let go of the handles, and step out of the machine.

Many machines also provide resistance over a longer range of motion for each exercise than is possible with free weights. In some cases, this resistance is balanced to meet theoretical "strength curves" of each muscle group being worked, something else free weights can't do for you.

On the negative side, machines are *very* expensive in comparison to free weights. For example, a machine setup for only one or two exercises per body part may cost up to $20,000. By contrast, you can set up a great home gym with free weights and related apparatus for only about $500. Therefore, the only place it's feasible to use machines is in a commercial gym.

The other main problem with machines is that it takes an incredible array of them to provide several exercises for each body part. While you might be able to do only four to six movements for your arms on a particular brand of machine, for example, you could probably come up with scores of exercises for each of the muscle groups using free weights and associated equipment. Doing the same four to six movements over and over again naturally will make pure machine training quite boring in the long run, which in turn will cut into any potential gains you might make from using the machines.

Ideally, you should combine both machines and free weights in your workouts. And you should take advantage of every brand of machine available to you in the gym where you train. Over the long haul, you'll achieve the most complete development by using the greatest number of different types of training apparatus.

In my own workouts, I utilize every type of machine that Steve and I have in our gym, as well as every other type I happen to encounter when I'm training at other gyms while on the road. I also make extensive use of barbells, dumbbells, a wide variety of benches, chinning bars, dipping bars, and the entire gamut of cable systems. Machines or free weights? I like them both!

HOLISTIC TRAINING

Most of my muscle mass was developed through heavy workouts on basic exercises during my powerlifting period. Much of my muscle detail, on the other hand, was developed via lighter bodybuilding-training sessions slanted more towards isolation movements. As a result of these two types of training, I've developed a proportionately balanced, symmetrical, massive, and highly detailed physique.

I am atypical of most top bodybuilders, however. Rather than first developing mass and then going for detail, the way I did, most bodybuilders do both simultaneously. They combine heavy basics in their workouts with lighter isolation work, usually doing low reps for basics and higher reps for isolation work.

If you are confused about the difference between basic and isolation exercises, I'll define them for you. A basic movement is one in which large muscle groups are worked in concert with other major and/or minor body parts. In contrast, an isolation exercise is one in which stress is placed on a single muscle group or even a part of one complex. A chart of the best basic and isolation exercises for each body part follows.

The Best Basic and Isolation Exercises

Body Part	Basic Exercises	Isolation Exercises
Legs	Squats, Leg Presses, Stiff-Legged Deadlifts, Front Squats, Hack Squats	Leg Extensions, Leg Curls, Leg Adductions/Abductions
Back (traps)	Upright Rows (barbells, cable)	Shrugs (barbell, dumbbells, machines)
Back (lats)	Barbell/Dumbbell/Cable Rows, Chins, Pull-Downs	Stiff-Arm Pull-Downs, various types of Pullovers
Back (erectors)	Deadlifts	Hyperextensions
Chest	Incline/Flat/Decline Presses (barbell, dumbbells, machine), Parallel Bar Dips	Incline/Flat/Decline Flyes (dumbbells, cables, machine)
Shoulders	Overhead Presses, all types of presses for chest, Upright Rows	Front/Side/Bent Laterals (dumbbells, cables, machines), Barbell Front Raises
Biceps	Chins, Pull-Downs, all rowing exercises, all Barbell Curls	Concentration Curls (barbell, dumbbell), Machine Curls, Cable Curls, Preacher Curls (barbell/dumbbells/cable)
Triceps	Parallel Bar Dips, Close-Grip Benches, all types of presses	Push-Downs, all types of Triceps Extensions (barbell/dumbbell/cable/machine)
Forearms	Reverse Curls	Wrist Curls (barbell/dumbbell/cable), Reverse Wrist Curls (barbell/dumbbell/cable)
Calves	Jumping Squats	all types of Calf Raises
Abdominals	all types of Sit-Ups and Leg Raises	all types of Crunches

The only way to optimize your physical development is by training holistically. By this, I mean including all types of exercises, poundages, rep ranges, and training apparatus in your workouts *over a period of time*.

Most successful competitors train in cycles. During the off-season, they work towards gaining greater muscle mass by doing short, heavy, basic low-rep workouts. Prior to a show, they work towards gaining greater muscle detail by doing longer isolation work and higher reps. They also do transitional cycles between off-season and precontest phases—cycles that meld the two types of workouts. Thus, over the span of a year, they train holistically.

You can be holistic in your workouts either by training in cycles or by shifting your exercise style over a period of a few days, a week, or a few weeks. Although both approaches are valid, experimentation will ultimately reveal which type of holistic training works best for you. Once you discover which works best, stick with it.

Sometimes it's a good idea to do holistic training in terms of sets, reps, and weights for one or more movement(s) in a single workout. This is best accomplished by using a half-pyramid or full-pyramid system for that exercise. The following are samples of both methods.

Half-Pyramid

SET NUMBER	% OF MAXIMUM LIFT	NUMBER OF REPS
1	50%	15
2	60%	12
3	70%	10
4	75%	8
5	80%	7
6	85%	6
7	90%	5

Full-Pyramid

SET NUMBER	% OF MAXIMUM LIFT	NUMBER OF REPS
1	50%	12
2	60%	10
3	70%	8
4	80%	6
5	90%	5
6	80%	6
7	70%	8
8	60%	10
9	50%	12

Generally, pyramiding works best in the off-season, when your energy levels have not

Demonstrating correct squatting form — beginning descent.

been depleted by a precontest diet, which makes you more vulnerable to injury. However, you really don't need to be afraid of injury from the heavy, low-rep sets because early in the pyramid the higher-rep sets with lighter weights will leave your joints and muscles thoroughly warmed up.

SPLIT ROUTINES

Early increases in training intensity generally come from a gradual increase in the total number of sets performed during each training session. Eventually, you will be doing so many sets that you won't have sufficient energy reserves to commit yourself totally to every set. Then, it's better to split your body's various muscles into equal groups and train only part of your body each session. This kind of program is called a split routine.

A split routine requires more than three workouts per week—usually four at first, later six, perhaps twice a day prior to competitions. Several examples of four-day split routines, the most basic type, follow.

Sample 4-Day Split Routines

VARIABLE 1

MONDAY AND THURSDAY	TUESDAY AND FRIDAY
Calves	Abs
Chest	Legs
Back	Upper Arms
Delts	Forearms

VARIABLE 2

MONDAY AND THURSDAY	TUESDAY AND FRIDAY
Abs	Abs
Back	Chest
Biceps	Shoulders
Legs	Triceps
Forearms	Calves

VARIABLE 3

MONDAY AND THURSDAY	TUESDAY AND FRIDAY
Abs	Chest
Legs	Shoulders
Back	Upper Arms
Calves	Forearms

As long as you rest at least 2 full days between workouts for each muscle group (usually with the exception of calves, abs, and forearms), a split routine will work well for you. Exercise physiologists have discovered that muscles must be rested at least 48 hours—preferably 72 hours—between workouts in order for them to fully recover from the previous session and increase in hypertrophy (size, tone, and strength). They have also determined through experiments that peak hypertrophy occurs between 3 and 4 days after a workout, and it begins to deteriorate 5 or 6 days following a specific body-part workout.

Therefore, most champion bodybuilders follow a 4-day cycle (3-on/1-off) split routine, in which they work each major muscle group every fourth day. Two sample 4-day cycle split routines follow.

Sample 4-Day Cycle Split Routines

ALTERNATIVE 1

DAY 1	DAY 2	DAY 3	DAY 4
Chest	Shoulders	Quads	Rest
Back	Upper Arms	Hamstrings	
Calves	Forearms	Abs	

ALTERNATIVE 2

DAY 1	DAY 2	DAY 3	DAY 4
Chest	Upper Back	Abs	Rest
Shoulders	Biceps	Quads	
Triceps	Forearms	Hamstrings	
Calves	Abs	Lower Back	

Prior to a competition, when your energy reserves are low, you might even wish to train twice each day—a practice that limits the duration of your workouts by allowing you to take rest periods between your sessions. This is called a double-split routine, and it's discussed in detail in Chapter 6.

SUPERSETS

A common way of increasing training intensity is to do supersets, or two successive movements (with minimal rest between), followed by a nor-

Chins — start.

mal rest interval of 60 to 120 seconds. These two-exercise compounds are most frequently used prior to a competition, but high-level bodybuilders do supersets year-round.

The most fundamental type of superset is done with one exercise for two antagonistic muscle groups—such as biceps and triceps, forearm flexors and forearm extensors, or quadriceps and hamstrings. The following are examples of supersets for those three antagonistic groupings of body parts:

> Biceps + Triceps: Barbell Curls + Pulley Push-Downs
> Forearm Flexors + Extensors: Wrist Curls + Reverse Wrist Curls
> Quads + Hamstrings: Leg Extensions + Leg Curls

A more intense type of superset involves compounding two movements for the same body part. This method works best for larger and more complex muscle groups—such as those in the legs, back, or chest. The following are examples of supersets for a single body part:

> Quads: Squats + Leg Extensions
> Hamstrings: Stiff-Legged Deadlifts + Leg Curls
> Back: Barbell Bent Rows + Lat Machine Pull-Downs
> Chest: Bench Presses + Flat-Bench Flyes
> Delts: Overhead Presses + Side Laterals

Particularly weak minor-muscles groups, such as biceps or triceps, can also be trained with supersets. Here are examples of supersets for them:

> Biceps: Barbell Preacher Curls + Barbell Curls
> Triceps: Close-Grip Bench Presses + Lying Triceps Extensions

PRE-EXHAUSTION SUPERSETS

A common problem with many bodybuilders is an inability to make good gains in torso muscle mass—such as in the lats, traps, pecs, and delts. Frequently this occurs either because the arm muscles are so disproportionately strong that they take over much of the load with basic torso exercises—such as Bench Presses, Barbell Bent Rows, and Overhead Presses—or when the upper-arm muscles are so weak that they collapse from fatigue on basic torso movements before the lats, pecs, delts, or traps are sufficiently fatigued to grow optimally.

When weak arms are preventing proper torso development, you can overcome the problem by using pre-exhaustion supersets, which temporarily render the torso muscles *weaker* than the arms. This is accomplished by first doing an isolation exercise for a particular torso muscle group, followed immediately by a basic movement for the same body part. The isolation exercise temporarily makes the torso group weaker than normal—and if a basic movement immediately follows, the upper-arm muscles will be briefly so strong in comparison to the torso group that you will be able to push the torso body part exceptionally hard with the basic exercise.

Never allow more than about 5 seconds to elapse between the exercises of a pre-exhaustion superset, however. After only 10 to 12 seconds, a pre-exhausted muscle will have recouped 50 percent of its strength and energy reserves. Therefore, the rest interval between supersetted movements should be kept to an absolute minimum.

These are some sample pre-exhaustion supersets for various torso muscle groups:

    Chest (in general): Flat-Bench Flyes + Bench Presses
    Chest (upper): Incline Flyes + Incline Presses
    Chest (lower): Decline Flyes + Decline Presses
    Delts: Dumbbell Side Laterals + Overhead Presses
    Delts: Upright Rows + Dumbbell Presses
    Traps: Barbell Shrugs + Upright Rows
    Lats: Stiff-Arm Pulldowns + Chins
    Lats: Cross-Bench Dumbbell Pullovers + Lat Pulldowns

Chins — finish.

Incline Dumbbell Presses — start/finish.

Incline Dumbbell Presses — midpoint.

Many bodybuilders have been able to eliminate serious deficiencies in torso muscle development over the years by using the pre-exhaustion technique. I'm sure it will work well for you, too. Just break into it slowly, and don't exceed about 5 total supersets for each torso muscle group.

BREAKING PLATEAUS

Regardless of how hard or consistently you work out, your body will respond in spurts when it comes to increases in muscle mass. Periods of rapid muscle growth lasting 2 to 4 weeks are generally followed by dormant phases lasting 2 or 3 weeks. But when you have failed to make gains for 5 or 6 weeks in a row, you undoubtedly have encountered a progress plateau, which you will need to break so that you can begin to make good gains again.

Progress plateaus can occur naturally, but they are most frequently caused by illness, by becoming overtrained, or by allowing yourself to get into training ruts. Overtraining was discussed earlier in this chapter, and health problems can be confirmed or disproved by your physician—but what about training ruts?

Very few bodybuilders can make consistent gains when following the same routine for long periods of time. By this, I mean performing the same exercises, sets, and reps, using the same training poundages and lengths of rest intervals. After a few weeks, mental boredom sets in—followed by physical boredom, followed by a cessation of muscle-mass gains.

I should point out, however, that there *are* a few bodybuilders with personalities that are conducive to following the same routine year after year and they still manage to make consistent gains. One such bodybuilder is seven-time Mr. Olympia Arnold Schwarzenegger, who followed the same training program the final 8 or 9 years of his competitive career.

The obvious way to avoid getting into training ruts is by changing your routine at regular intervals. I personally suggest moving on to a new program after you've been doing a routine for 6 weeks or less. On the other hand, many bodybuilders find it's best to follow a sort of non-routine, in which they perform a completely different workout for each body part every time they train it. Some bodybuilders call this technique *muscle-confusion* training.

During your first couple of years of steady training, you should experiment with following a set routine for various lengths of time, noting how quickly you reach plateaus. If you plateau out at the 8-week point, change routines every 6 weeks in order to avoid the problem. If you reach a plateau after only a week, try using a different routine for each bodybuilding workout.

Plateaus can also occur when you fail to progressively increase training intensity—either through increased training weights or by intensification techniques such as forced reps, cheating, supersets, and so forth. In this case, you can break a plateau merely by juicing up the intensity level of your workouts. If you increase intensity, you will increase muscle mass—it's that simple.

Poor mental attitude can also result in progress plateaus. This topic is discussed extensively in Chapter 5.

INDIVIDUALIZING ROUTINES

If you read a lot of bodybuilding books and muscle magazines, you can pick up numerous training programs, which are possible to follow for years at a time. But you won't make the same type of gains following a routine someone else made up as you could following one you carefully tailored to the unique requirements of your own body.

From personal experience and plenty of reading, you can gradually learn the mechanics of writing your own training programs; however, the following rules will certainly speed up the process.

- *Do not train too frequently.* For most young bodybuilders, a 4-day split routine will cause them to thoroughly stimulate their muscles, and then give them sufficient recovery time to allow hypertrophy. Even the most advanced competition-level bodybuilders will make their best gains on a three-on/one-off routine. Don't be seduced into training any more frequently.

• *Always work arm muscles after those torso muscles that require the same arm muscles to exert in basic movements.* The reason for this rule was explained in the section on pre-exhaustion supersets.

• *Generally, work from the larger muscle groups down to the smaller body parts when formulating a routine.* It should be fairly obvious that the larger muscle groups require more energy when trained properly than the small body parts. And it's much easier to work a small muscle group when you're beginning to run out of gas towards the end of a workout.

• *Train forearms last in any routine.* Once you've worked your forearms hard, you'll find it very difficult to grasp a barbell, dumbbell, or pulley handle comfortably.

• *Never train calves prior to thighs.* If you do, you'll find that your legs will shake so much that you will not be able to do heavy squats or even heavy leg presses.

• *Program basic exercises for each muscle group first in your routine, followed by isolation movements.* As with the large-to-small body parts rule, more energy is required to perform basic exercises than isolation movements. So, do basics first.

• *Hold down total sets.* I gave you upper thresholds of total sets for each body part at various bodybuilding-experience levels earlier in this chapter. Don't exceed them, or you'll risk overtraining.

• *Always include time for warm-ups.* Neglecting warm-ups drastically increases your chance of injury, so get into the habit of making time for them.

• *Find a consistent time each day for your workouts.* If you train at the same time each workout day, your body will adapt to the schedule by peaking energy levels for that time period.

By keeping these nine rules in mind, you should have little difficulty creating programs personally designed for your unique body. Be sure to include those exercises, movement sequences, sets, reps, and poundage schedules that experience has shown work best for your physique. And finally, be sure to listen to your body, because it will give you signals as to how good a particular training program happens to be. Your body is the best barometer.

4

EFFECTIVE BODYBUILDING NUTRITION

What you eat can affect your progress as a bodybuilder just as much as how you train. Most of the champs agree that nutrition and training are of equal importance during the off-season cycle, when they are pushing to increase their general muscle mass. Most also tend to feel that the closer they come to a competition, the greater the importance of proper nutrition, until diet becomes at least 90 percent of the battle during the final precontest week.

Novice bodybuilders, however, tend to focus all of their attention on their gym workouts, almost ignoring the nutritional aspect of the sport. Frequently, the signal that someone is becoming really hardcore is a sudden interest in bodybuilding nutrition. True hardcore bodybuilders—those training for competition-level muscle mass and muscularity—tend to be almost obsessed about what and when they eat.

The more quickly you become conscious of your diet, the more quickly you will start making championship gains in muscular development. Towards that end, here are 11 basic rules of good bodybuilding nutrition, which you can immediately implement in your diet.

• *Consume a small amount of animal protein at each daily meal.* In contrast to vegetable proteins, animal-source proteins are of a much higher biological quality and are therefore more easily assimilated into muscle tissue in your body. Also, the human digestive system is capable of processing only 20 to 25 grams of protein per meal, so it's best to eat smaller meals with high-quality animal-source protein in each one.

• *Eat more than three times per day.* When you consume small meals, which are more efficiently digested, you will need to eat four to six times per day, rather than consume the normal two or three large meals most people eat each day. Eating smaller and more frequent meals will tend to keep your appetite under control and your blood sugar levels at a consistency high level, permitting high-intensity training sessions.

• *Avoid junk foods.* These include foods high in sugar, white flour, and fat content—such as pastries, ice cream, and fried foods. Soft drinks, beer, and hard alcohol are also classified as junk foods. All junk foods are very counterproductive when it comes to building high-quality muscle mass.

• *Eat the greatest possible variety of foods over a period of time.* Most people get into the habit of consuming the same 10 to 12 foods day in and day out, and this prevents their bodies from absorbing the full spectrum of available nutrients. It's much better to expand your list of foods to the absolute limit, constantly varying them and trying to avoid eating any one food more frequently than every 3 or 4 days.

• *Drink lots of pure water.* Water is the body's natural cleanser and solvent, and you need to drink plenty of it each day. I recommend at least eight to 10 glasses per day. It's preferable to drink either freshly filtered, spring, or distilled water, which are all free from pollutants that might poison your system.

• *Consume a small quantity of vegetable-source fat each day.* Fat is a necessary nutrient for nerve health, as well as for the healthy appearance of your hair and skin. But animal fats—from meat, eggs, and milk—are bad for the body since they can cause cardiac disease and a variety of other ills. Therefore, you should obtain your fats from unsaturated vegetable sources—such as oils, grains, beans, and corn. (Avoid coconut oil, however, because it contains saturated fat that is just as bad for your body as animal fats.)

• *Base much of your diet around fresh fruits, vegetables, and salads, as well as grains, seeds, and nuts.* These foods are the highest in natural vitamin and mineral content, and should always make up at least 50 percent of your food bulk each day. They also taste

Diet and training are a 50—50 proposition in the off-season for hardcore bodybuilders. Just prior to a competition, however, diet is 80 to 90 percent responsible for success or failure onstage.

good, so you should not have much difficulty eating them.

• *Avoid using salt on your food.* One of the main components of table salt is sodium, which retains at least 50 times its weight in water inside the human body. To avoid harmful and unsightly bloating, top bodybuilders avoid consuming all sodium except that which occurs naturally in foods. They even try to avoid foods, such as celery, that are naturally high in sodium content.

• *Do not consume alcohol.* This recommendation is one that frequently upsets bodybuilders, particularly those who like to go out for a few brews after a workout. But drinking alcohol is counterproductive to bodybuilding success since alcohol is a depressant, provides empty calories, and robs the body of vitamin B.

• *Limit consumption of animal fats, and fats in general.* I've already mentioned the health hazards of consuming animal fats. Fats in general are more than twice as rich a source of calories as proteins or carbohydrates, so they tend to increase body-fat stores, blurring out hard-earned muscularity. Later in this chapter, you'll learn how to reduce body-fat levels by severely limiting fat intake. Even in the off-season, you should avoid consuming so much fat that you increase your body weight more than 10 pounds above off-season levels.

• *Use food supplements as insurance against nutritional deficiencies.* At a minimum, you should consume one multipack of vitamins, minerals, and trace elements each day to guard against progress-stalling nutritional deficiencies. For the best assimilation, vitamin and mineral supplements should be taken with meals. To improve the protein content of your diet, you can use free-form amino acid capsules, which should be taken about 30 minutes before a meal.

THE SEARCH

Bodybuilding nutrition is a highly complex subject, which continues to grow more complex each year as new information is discovered. This chapter is a good starting point in mastering the subject, but you'll need to do a lot more reading if you want to learn enough about nutrition to become a champion bodybuilder.

Several books have been written specifically about bodybuilding diet, and virtually all muscle magazines carry articles each issue on the topic. There are also literally hundreds of nutrition books, both general and on specific topics, that you can also use to help increase your knowledge.

I simply can't emphasize enough the importance of learning as much as possible about bodybuilding nutrition. Your degree of knowledge—and what you do with it—will literally make or break you as a competitive bodybuilder.

THE CYCLE-DIETING PRINCIPLE

The cycle-training principle is widely accepted and followed in competitive bodybuilding. During the off-season, hardcore bodybuilders train less frequently each week than in a peaking cycle, work with heavier weights and lower repetitions, and do fewer total sets for each body part—all in an effort to promote maximum recovery between workouts and thereby build an optimum amount of muscle mass. If they have a particular weak point, they will also do specific training to improve that area during the off-season.

Two or three months prior to competition, serious bodybuilders begin to make a transition from off-season to precontest training by gradually increasing the number of workouts per week (often even double-splitting, if time allows) and the total amount of work performed for each muscle group. They also add repetitions, and kick in such training-intensification techniques as supersets, forced reps, descending sets, and iso-tension to further the peaking effort. Finally,

Shrugs demonstrated on machine.

they do considerably more aerobic training, which mobilizes and burns off stored body fat—eventually revealing a massive and highly muscular physique onstage.

Just as there is a cycle-training principle, there is a cycle-dieting principle—which involves oscillations between off-season building cycles and precontest peaking cycles, as well as appropriate transitional phases. In general, bodybuilders eat more food in the off-season, allowing them to train heavy and hard, and increase muscle mass and weight. In the precontest peaking phase, they induce a caloric deficit in order to burn off all vestiges of excess fat. Off-season and precontest dietary cycles are discussed in detail in the next two sections.

OFF-SEASON DIET

Once you have trained a muscle group heavily, you must have sufficient amino acids in your bloodstream during your recovery cycle to induce an increase in muscle mass. To ensure that you have sufficient amino acids in your system, you must induce your digestive tract to process more protein than is possible under normal circumstances.

A little earlier, I commented on the body's inability to digest more than 20 to 25 grams of protein during each meal. Assuming you could process 25 grams each time you ate, three meals per day would add up to about 75 total grams of protein digested. But by eating more frequently—say, six times per day—you can force more aminos into your system. Over six meals, you would make available for assimilation 150 grams of protein each day.

During an off-season building cycle, it is essential for you to eat more than three meals per day. Ideally, you should consume six or seven at approximate 2-hour intervals, but four or five would be better than three. These meals must each contain at least 20 grams of animal-source protein, plus plenty of complex carbohydrates to fuel your workout energy requirements.

Complex carbohydrates are more slowly digested than simple carbs, such as fruit or refined sugar, and give you a more sustained flow of energy. Simple carbs tend to cause peaks and valleys in energy flow. The valleys are lower than what you can really endure and still be able to work out with peak intensity. So, always concentrate on complex carbs rather than simple carbohydrates, and try to avoid as much refined sugar as you can in the off-season.

What are the best complex-carbohydrate foods? My favorites are potatoes, rice, yams, pasta, grains, seeds, and vegetables. About the only time I'll eat a piece of fruit for actual workout energy is before I start a training session.

Given the foregoing factors, here is a sample off-season menu that you can adapt to your own tastes in individual foods:

Meal 1 (8:00 a.m.): cheese omelet, oatmeal, nonfat milk, and multipack

Meal 2 (10:00 a.m.): tuna salad, rice, nonfat milk, and B-complex vitamins

Meal 3 (12:00 a.m.): broiled chicken breast (no skin), baked yam, green vegetable, nonfat milk, and B-complex vitamins

Meal 4 (2:00 p.m.): scrambled eggs, ground beef patty, green salad, nonfat milk, and vitamin C

Meal 5 (4:00 p.m.): protein drink, and B-complex vitamins

Workout (4:30–6:30 p.m.)

Meal 6 (7:00 p.m.): broiled lean ground beef, baked potato, green vegetable, nonfat milk, and vitamin C

Meal 7 (11:00 p.m.): hard-boiled eggs, hard cheese, or cottage cheese, and nonfat milk

As you have probably noted, milk is a staple in off-season weight-gaining diets. Some people can't handle milk, however, usually because of lack of enzyme lactase (which digests lactose, the sugar in milk) in their digestive tracts. If you have this problem, you can substitute either fruit juice, coffee, iced tea, or ice water for the milk. You'll probably still be able to eat cheese, cottage cheese, and other processed milk products, because the lactose is eliminated in the processing.

B-complex vitamins are also essential when attempting to gain muscular body weight because they stimulate the appetite and help to increase tissue. Since B-complex vitamins are all water-soluble, they must be taken periodically throughout the day.

Learn to cook as a bodybuilder, using a minimum amount of oil and little or no sodium. Baking, broiling, boiling, and frying in a nonstick pan are the best ways to prepare meat.

PRECONTEST DIET

There are two main schools of thought when it comes to ripping up for a contest dietarily. The least popular is to limit carbohydrate intake. But since a low-carb diet is mentally and physically grueling and always results in a loss of muscle tissue, most competitive bodybuilders these days follow a low-fat/low-calorie diet.

Earlier, I stated that fat is more than twice as concentrated a source of stored energy as protein or carbohydrates. The actual figures are about nine calories per gram of fat versus about four calories per gram of protein or carbohydrate.

Therefore, you can easily induce a caloric deficit by systematically replacing fat in your diet with either protein or carbohydrate. Over a period of 2 or 3 months, you can gradually reduce the fat content in your diet—thereby lowering the total amount of calories consumed each day—and systematically strip away all fat obscuring your muscles. When correctly timed, this process can result in a highly muscular-looking physique onstage at contest time.

When I diet for a competition, the process is one long crescendo in which I diet ever more strictly each passing week. However, I don't just gradually reduce the total number of calories consumed each day; it's a much more complex process than that, since I jump my caloric consumption upwards and downwards in an effort to fake out my mind and body, while still reducing the *average* number of calories consumed each day.

There is a reason for this oscillation upwards and downwards in calories from one day to the next. If the body is systematically fed the same number of calories, and that number is far below the amount needed to maintain your body weight, your mind will perceive this process as something akin to actual starvation. When this happens, the mind basically tells the body to hang on to all of its fat stores as tenaciously as possible, making it very difficult for you to reduce body-fat levels. But when the calories are increased and decreased from day to day, the mind doesn't perceive a diet as a starvation situation.

Let me give you an example of how I might fluctuate calorie intake. Let's say I've been taking in about 1,200 calories per day for a few days. When it gets tough to maintain that level, I'll drop to 800 or 900 calories for one day, and then jump up to 1,500 or 1,600 for the next day or two, which feels like feasting in comparison. So, in essence, while I've averaged 1,200 calories a day, I've actually been consuming a wide spectrum of calories.

I have to be careful not to lose muscle tissue when I'm on 800 to 900 calories per day, so I use ketone test strips (available in pharmacies without a prescription) to periodically test my urine. If the strip turns light pink, I can tell that I'm going into ketosis, which is a good indication that my body is beginning to lose muscle. When this happens, I jump my calories upwards immediately. Using the ketone strips makes the process much more scientific by taking out all the guesswork.

The following are 10 widely accepted rules for limiting fat intake in your diet when peaking out for a show.

- *Never fry foods*. Whenever you fry a food, some of the oil used in the pan is soaked up in the meat at a rate of about 100 calories per tablespoon. You should also avoid sautéing meat, or wok cooking in which oil is used. It's better to bake, broil, or boil all of your meats.

- *Choose meat according to fat content*. The fattiest meats are pork, beef, and lamb, which are referred to as red meat. Red meat is higher in fat than white meats, such as fish, chicken, and turkey. Poultry is higher in fat content than fish. And various types of fish are higher in fat than others.

- *Avoid full-fat milk products*. You can consume nonfat milk and milk products and thereby substantially reduce the caloric content of what you eat. For the final few weeks prior to competition, you will probably wish to eliminate milk products altogether, since they contain an enzyme that causes bloating in most people.

- *Drop out the fatty yolks when you eat eggs.* Egg whites are a superior source of protein prior to competition because they contain no fat at all. In contrast, egg yolks are largely fat. As a competition approaches, you should drop more and more yolks from your egg dishes, until over the last weeks you are consuming only the egg whites.

- *Do not use oily commercial salad dressings.* There are many salad dressings available from health food suppliers in which most or all of the oil has been eliminated. Or, you can use vinegar and/or lemon juice as an alternative.

- *Use herbs and spices in cooking.* Each time you use a new herb or spice, you add a new taste to a dish without increasing calories. Constantly experiment with new tastes in food to keep your diet interesting. You can also broil food over an open wood fire to enhance the taste; mesquite adds a particularly interesting flavor.

- *Avoid bread high in fat or butter.* If you include bread in your precontest diet, buy it from a health food outlet. This way, you can select bread without a lot of butter or oil, both of which add calories and are used extensively in bread from commercial bakeries.

- *Eat baked potatoes dry.* The toppings are what makes baked potatoes high in fat calories. Also, you'll be able to enjoy the delicate flavor of the potato more if you don't top it with butter or sour cream. The same rule applies to other tubers—such as yams—in your diet.

- *Avoid boiling vegetables.* When you boil vegetables, many of their nutrients are lost in the cooking process. And virtually everyone adds oil to the pot when boiling veggies, in order to keep them from sticking to the sides.

- *Consume safe snacks.* Whenever you start craving foods—which always happens during a precontest diet—you can relieve the cravings by consuming high-sugar fruits, such as watermelon, peaches, or nectarines. These foods will satisfy your cravings efficiently without substantially adding calories to your diet.

To show you how I personally eat during off-season and precontest cycles, I've included my meal plans for both phases on pages 96–97.

PRECONTEST WATER BALANCING

If you thoroughly understand how both sodium and carbohydrate attract water to themselves, then you can manipulate their intake to dramatically improve the hardness and general appearance of your physique over the final week before a competition.

Sodium attracts and holds more than 50 times its weight in water within your body—water that will blur out your best cuts and cause you to look puffy and bloated.

Carbohydrate, on the other hand, attracts much less water—approximately four times its weight. However, if the carbohydrate happens to be in your muscles when it attracts its water, your muscles will appear artificially—and briefly—larger than normal. And, if the carbohydrate is in your vascular system when it attracts its water, it will fill out your bloodstream and cause you to appear markedly more vascular than usual.

The trick is to manipulate the water content in various parts of your body so that you fill those areas that make your physique look better conditioned without also filling the areas beneath the skin and within the abdomen—where the water would make you appear smooth and would bloat your midsection, causing you to look like you had just swallowed a barrel of beer. But if you correctly apply the processes called sodium loading-depletion and carbohydrate depletion-loading discussed in this section, you should have no difficulty directing the water to precisely where you want it to go.

Fluid replacement during a workout is essential, because lowered fluid volume and electrolyte depletion cause unnecessary fatigue. Plain water is best, along with a tablet containing the electrolyte minerals.

Even though these processes should work well for you, keep in mind that every body reacts differently to various external stimuli. Therefore, you should experiment primarily during the off-season—but also during one or two peaks, in order to make precise determinations when you're in top shape—to see if you need to vary the suggested amounts of each nutrient and/or the lengths of time you should be ingesting it.

Excess water retention on contest day is one of the biggest problems confronting inexperienced women competitors. This can come from menstrual timing, but it's more frequently a reaction to the stress associated with stepping onstage. Stress causes the hormone aldosterone to be released in large quantities, and aldosterone contributes to water retention.

The process of sodium loading-depletion can free you of the problems caused by aldosterone secretion. It will also help you actually flush the water that normally occurs in healthy people out from under your skin. This process takes one week, in which you consume more than the usual amount of sodium for 4 days and then take in absolutely no sodium at all for the final 3 days.

The amount of sodium you consume when loading is basically dependent on relative body mass—the larger you are, the more you should take. An average-sized women should start out by taking two full grams of sodium the seventh day from a competition, three the next day, four the next, and five the final loading day. Then for the final 72 hours prior to the competition, she should completely limit her sodium intake, getting it as effectively close to zero as possible.

You'll need a book on nutrition in order to tell which foods are almost devoid of sodium. Some foods have much more sodium than you would think. During this time, you'll probably even want to switch from eating fish from the sea to eating freshwater fish, such as trout. (Frozen trout are usually available and are practically free of sodium.)

Although you should avoid sodium for the last 3 days, you might want to experiment with consuming 100 to 200 milligrams of sodium on the day of your competition. For some athletes, this helps fill out the vascular system and tighten the skin. But if you take in too much, you'll undoubtedly smooth out; so, it's essential to try this once or twice to see how it works for you and precisely how much works best.

When you are sodium-loading and carb-depleting, you will look pretty bad during the first 5 or 6 days of the final week leading up to a show. You will be puffy from taking in sodium and flat-looking from depleting carbs. But if you keep firmly in mind that you'll look great on contest day if you stick it out, you won't be tempted to drop out of the competition.

The process of carbohydrate depletion-loading is based on a principle called supercompensations, discovered during the 1960s by Scandinavian exercise physiologists. It was originally developed to increase energy stores for endurance runners, but it works well for bodybuilders, too. This is because it packs more sugar than normal into the muscles, liver, and bloodstream—which in turn attracts water and makes you appear bigger, harder, and more vascular.

Carb depletion-loading is generally a 5- or 6-day cycle, and, as with sodium loading-depletion, you must experiment with every variable to see which ones work best for you.

For the first 3 days, you should consume a bare minimum of carbohydrate—certainly less than 50 grams per day. (Most bodybuilders on this regimen find that they need to limit their carb intake to under 20 grams a day.) Combined with plenty of gym and aerobics workouts, 3 days of consuming limited carbohydrates will effectively deplete your system of all sugars.

I won't try to kid you by saying that you'll feel great and look good when you are carb-depleting. With your brain starved of sugar, you may feel downright depressed and paranoid at times and your energy levels undoubtedly will be very low. But you have to suffer a little for this system to work.

Over the final 2 or 3 days prior to competition, you need to take in a minimum of 180 to 200 grams of complex carbs (*never* use simple-carbohydrate foods when you're loading) to

It's particularly grueling to get in a hard workout when you're on a precontest diet. But the athletes who can force themselves to keep pushing hard when they're fatigued have the best chance of eventually becoming champions.

Vitamins, minerals, protein powders, and amino acid capsules provide foolproof insurance against progress-stalling dietary deficiencies.

replenish your body-sugar stores. If you've depleted correctly, your body will supercompensate by packing in even more body sugar than normal. You'll probably find that it's best to nibble all day on potatoes and rice when loading, rather than trying to pack all that carbohydrate into three or four large meals. Also, nibbling all day will help you keep your stomach flat.

While you can make some of your experiments with sodium and carb loading during the off-season, you will probably have to try it during several peaks for minor contests in order to see how you appear in contest shape. When you do finally get all of the variables down pat, you'll find that all excess water will be sucked out from under your skin and into your muscles and vascular system, making you appear in better shape than normally possible.

One thing I'd better caution you against is trying to dehydrate your body by using chemical diuretics. This is very risky from a health standpoint, and, after taking a diuretic, you'll find that it actually makes you appear flat and unimpressive. It's a much better practice to time your training and dietary preparations so that you will be in shape by your competition, without having to catch up by using diuretics.

FOOD SUPPLEMENTATION

Most competitive bodybuilders use plenty of food supplements to improve their gains. If you don't take in enough vitamins, minerals, and amino acids, you will fail to make good gains, regardless of how you train. Your health will not be in the type of peak you need to build up your muscles, and you won't have the necessary nutrients in your bloodstream to actually form new muscle tissue.

Since food supplements are costly, you should be aware of what it takes to get the best deal when you walk into a health food shop. First, you'll need to learn how to critically read labels on food-supplement containers. Each one includes the potency of every nutrient listed as well as the amount of units (tablets, capsules, ounces, grams) in the container. Compare potencies from one container to another; then purchase the supplement with the best potencies at the most reasonable price.

You'll also find out that some supplement companies are more reputable than others. Usually you will discover this by talking with other bodybuilders at the gym or backstage at competitions. After a while, however, you will be forming your own judgments according to how well each supplement works for you.

Which supplements should you buy? At first, you should probably use a good-quality multipack of vitamins, minerals, and trace elements. This multipack should be taken early in the day with a meal. Later, you can begin to experiment with individual vitamins and minerals. I'd suggest trying them in this order: B-complex, C, calcium, magnesium, potassium, E, and then anything else you've heard about from other bodybuilders or read about in bodybuilding books and magazines.

Protein and/or amino-acid supplementation is also important. Start out by using a milk-and-egg protein powder, which you can mix up in a blender with additional milk and some type of soft fruit for flavoring. This protein drink should be taken between meals, not in place of or along with normal food at mealtime.

Free-form and branched-chain amino acids are much more expensive but also more effective than concentrated protein powders. They work very well in helping to pack on lean body mass. Try taking them about 30 minutes prior to each meal or any time you feel tired, sleepy, or slightly hungry.

It will probably take at least a year or two for you to come up with a personalized program of food supplementation, but it will be worth your effort. Combined with a good solid diet of normal foods, supplements can help boost you to new and higher levels of muscular development.

MY PERSONAL MEAL PLANS

OFF-SEASON

Breakfast: oatmeal with raisins, honey, wheat germ, and ¼ cup nonfat milk; three egg whites and one yolk scrambled (sometimes with cheese); two slices whole-wheat toast with jam; and coffee

Midmorning: banana and coffee

Lunch: stir-fried chicken and mixed vegetables, steamed rice, homemade bran muffin, and coffee

Midafternoon: protein drink (nonfat milk or juice, protein powder, strawberries or blueberries, and ice)

Supper: 10 oz. fish or 6 oz. steak, baked potato, steamed vegetables, sugar-free jello with cooked peaches or apples, and coffee

Snack: toasted bagel with honey or jam, and hot chocolate

Approximate calories: 2,600

SUPPLEMENTS:

Multipack of vitamins/minerals	1/day
Vitamin C (1,000 mg.)	4/day
Vitamin B-complex (100 mg.)	3/day
Amino acids (capsules)	6/day
Desiccated liver	6/day

PRECONTEST

DAY ONE

Breakfast: oatmeal with cinnamon and Equal, four-egg-white omelet with chopped onion, and coffee with Sweet 'n' Low

Snack: banana and coffee

Lunch: 5 oz. chicken breast (skinned and broiled), two slices diet whole-wheat bread, ½ cup steamed carrots, 1 cup broccoli, and coffee

Snack: Large dry baked potato, and coffee

Supper: 8 oz. broiled haddock, 1 cup steamed peas, ½ cup corn, 1 cup steamed rice, 1 cup fresh strawberries, and coffee

Snack: Two rice cakes, 1 tablespoon jam, and coffee

Approximate calories: 1,600

DAY TWO

Breakfast: shredded wheat with Equal and ½ cup nonfat milk, four-egg-white omelet with green peppers, and coffee

Snack: apple and coffee

Lunch: small can of tuna with diet dressing, two slices diet bread, lettuce and tomato salad, and coffee

Snack: banana and coffee

Supper: 5 oz. chicken breast, ½ cup steamed cauliflower, ½ cup steamed green beans, ½ cup steamed rice, and coffee

Snack: ½ cup pasta with tomato sauce

Approximate calories: 1,500

DAY THREE (LOW-CARB DAY)

Breakfast: eight-egg-white omelet with chopped onion, and coffee

Snack: small can of tuna, rice cake, and coffee

Lunch: 4 oz. steamed chicken, 1 cup steamed broccoli, and coffee

Snack: 4 oz. turkey breast, and coffee

Supper: 4 oz. shrimp, ½ cup low-fat cottage cheese, and coffee

Snack: 6 oz. halibut with lettuce, cucumber, and tomato; and coffee

Approximate calories: 1,100
(30 grams of carbohydrate)

SUPPLEMENTS:

Multipack of vitamins/minerals	1/day
Vitamin C (1,000 mg.)	6/day
Total B (at least 100 mg. of each individual B-complex vitamin)	4/day
Multiple mineral	6/day
L-carnitine	2,000 mg./day
Inosine	1,500 mg./day*
Amino acids	16/day
Desiccated liver	16/day

*Inosine only on training days

APPROXIMATE MEAL TIMES:

- 11 a.m. (I get to bed after midnight due to obligations with our gym.)
- 1 p.m.
- 3 p.m.
- 5:30 p.m.
- 8:30 p.m.
- 11:30 p.m.

5
MIND MAGIC IN BODYBUILDING

Beneath the surface of any champion bodybuilder, you will always find an informally educated psychologist who knows exactly which mental-programming techniques assist her the most in improving her physique.

Many top bodybuilding champs have said that the mind is the body's "biggest muscle." I wholeheartedly agree with that statement, based upon my extensive experience in international track and field, as a six-time World Champion powerlifter, and as an IFBB Women's Pro World Champion bodybuilder.

For the sake of a convenient, easily understood illustration of mind power in bodybuilding, try thinking of your physique as a massive ocean liner and your mind as that ship's comparatively tiny rudder. When the rudder is moved even a fraction of a degree, a ship weighing thousands of tons is turned in the direction dictated by the tiny rudder. Your mind and body operate in a similar manner, with even the most subtle of mental shifts causing great changes in your self-confidence and general mental attitude—and, in turn, in your physique.

At first, you may think that the mental techniques I will teach you in this chapter are some type of New Age gibberish, but you're in for a big surprise. Once you've tried them out for a while, you will begin to see what overwhelming effect they will have on how your physique appears onstage at each successive competition.

POSITIVE THINKING

As owner-operator, with my husband, Steve, of our own hardcore bodybuilding gym, I am constantly impressed by the positive effects a good bodybuilding training-and-nutrition program can have on a woman. And I mean physical and mental. I often see shy little mice come into the gym, emerging a month or two later as lionesses! When you drastically improve your physical appearance and strength levels, it's impossible for your self-image not to soar, as well.

If a woman greatly improves her strength levels and muscle mass and tone—and becomes confident that she will continue to physically

improve herself—it's quite natural for her to take a positive attitude towards all of her life's endeavors. For example, the terror at applying for a new job often changes into buoyant self-confidence for the mouse-turned lioness. In almost every facet of her life, a physically superior woman thinks more and more positively as her physique improves.

We competitive bodybuilders take positive thinking way past the point where an average woman stops. Positive thinking—and the self-confidence it engenders—are the fuel we use to push our rocket ships to the moon!

Ideally, every woman bodybuilder should think positively 100 percent of the time. But ever since we have been very young, we have all been socialized in one way or another to think pessimistically. For instance, how many well-meaning young mothers have warned their daughters: "Now don't pump so high on that playground swing. You could fall off and hurt yourself."

If you sat down for a few minutes and thought of all the insidious ways you've been socialized to think negatively, you'd be astonished. Sometimes it seems like society is one big machine dedicated to promoting negativity. Don't you think it's time to reverse that trend and begin to think positively instead.

The easiest way to begin thinking positively on a regular basis is to consciously look for ways in which you think in a negative fashion, and then purposefully eliminate each of your negative thoughts as quickly as possible—banishing them from your mind for all eternity. You will probably find a written Negative Thought Journal helpful in facilitating this process; a sample page from such a journal follows.

In order to keep a Negative Thought Journal, you need to become conscious enough of your negative thoughts to actually be able to identify them. Then you need to work like mad to change negative to positive. After you've gone through this process over a number of months, you'll be thinking as positively as a Ms. Olympia finalist. I guarantee it!

Note: You can keep this type of Negative Thought Journal in any spiral-bound notebook with lined pages, or in a bound journal book. It can even be kept as part of your training diary.

Negative Thought Journal (Sample Page)

Negative Thought	Positive Counterpart	Date of Change
1. I just don't have enough time to train more than twice a week.	1. By rearranging my daily schedule, I can actually train hard 4 days a week.	4/21
2. I can't survive a day without eating chocolate. When I don't eat it, I get depressed.	2. Chocolate makes me fat. A good workout actually makes me feel better than an entire box of chocolates.	4/23
3. My bench press isn't going up because I'm afraid I'll injure myself if I go any heavier.	3. With a good warm-up, optimum form, and a good spotter, I can bench press the entire state of Maine without getting hurt!	4/24

THE GOAL-SETTING PROCESS

For optimum performance, every athlete—and this includes bodybuilders—needs a plan of attack, a roadmap to success. Goal setting provides such a roadmap. The faster you learn to set goals, reach these goals, and then set them again even higher, the more quickly you will arrive at competitive bodybuilding success.

An easy way to visualize goals is by seeing them as stepping stones across a broad, shallow brook. It's impossible to jump from one side of the brook to the other side, but you can certainly step across the brook one stone at a time. If you sequentially hop lightly from one stepping stone to the next, you will be across the brook in no time at all!

Most bodybuilders have short-range goals, long-range goals, and an ultimate goal. The *ultimate goal* is the one you should be shooting for over the full span of your competitive bodybuilding career. My own ultimate goal is to win the Ms. Olympia title, and no woman bodybuilder worth her salt should settle for anything less.

A step down from your ultimate goal are *long-range goals*. Unlike an ultimate goal, which is set only once, long-range goals are usually set once a year. After each Ms. Olympia competition, I like to rest for a week or two—primarily to allow my competitive emotions to subside—and then set my long-range goal for the following year. That particular long-term goal culminates with another Olympia, after which I set a newer and higher long-range goal for the next year.

There are many types of long-range goals. These are five of the most common:

- to win a higher title than ever before;

- to dramatically improve a weak body part, thereby perfecting the balance of physical proportions;

- to gain a certain amount of muscular body weight (for instance, 2 or 3 pounds in a year) without concurrently increasing the percentage of body fat;

- to dramatically improve stage presence and posing ability; and

- to maintain an optimum bodybuilding diet more consistently than ever before.

When power-training, the mental concentration factor becomes particularly intense. Prior to a set, I spend 20 to 30 seconds psyching up, preparing myself mentally and physically to complete the set as powerfully as possible.

A step down from long-range goals are *short-range goals*, which are commonly set at one-month intervals. The idea here is to set 12 smaller—and more easily reached—monthly goals that, when added up, produce the long-range goals you have set for that year. Perhaps the following example will make the goal-setting process easier to understand.

Let's say you have just placed fifth in your class at your State Championships. Obviously, you want to win both your class and the overall trophy the following year, so you set out to discover which weaknesses prevented you from winning your show this year. You politely ask the opinions of judges, experienced gym owners, respected coaches, physique photographers, and other people whom you consider to be unbiased experts. You also analyze every available photo of yourself from that show.

With all of this objective input, you discover that your upper body—your chest, back, delts, bis, tris, forearms, abs—are of almost National caliber. Even your calves are well-developed, although they're a few percentage points behind your upper body. What sunk your ship was your weak quadriceps, hamstrings, and gluteus maximus development. Bring up those three areas, and you'll have a great chance to win the whole enchilada next year.

The best way to improve your three weak areas is by doing heavy work on full Squats, Stiff-Legged Deadlifts, and Leg Curls (lying, seated, standing—they all work well). Let's set an arbitrary long-range goal over the course of the coming year of increasing your exercise weights (for reps, not a single effort) in the Squat by 100 pounds, in the Stiff-Legged Deadlifts by 100 pounds, and in the Leg Curls by 50 pounds. As long as you consistently use very strict biomechanics, increasing your weights in these three key exercises will dramatically increase muscle mass in your problem areas, balancing your proportions and (voilà!) winning you that State title you're after.

It probably sounds like a real job to add 100 pounds to your Squat or Stiff-Legged Deadlift in a year. But if you break it down to monthly increases of only 10 pounds on each movement, not only would it be manageable but you would end up with 120-pound increases at the end of the year! By the same token, adding 5 pounds per month on Leg Curls would increase your exercise poundage by 60 big ones! Of course, as several short-term goals can add up to a long-term goal, many of the long-term goals can eventually culminate in your ultimate goal.

However, it's always important to keep your goals realistic. It would be totally unrealistic, for instance, to believe that you could add an inch of new muscle mass to your upper arm measurement within the next year, regardless of how hard you train your biceps and triceps. And, if you are 7 feet tall, you might be better off setting goals in basketball than in bodybuilding.

As a final comment on goal-setting, let me quote the eminent Chinese philosopher Lao-tzu, who founded the Taoist religion over two millennia ago: "The journey of a thousand miles starts with a single step." Just keep putting one foot in front of the other, and you'll eventually walk a thousand miles. Likewise, set after set of heavy Standing Barbell Curls will ultimately give you the biceps of a Ms. Olympia or Pro World Champion.

CONCENTRATION

One aspect of bodybuilding mental approach that *always* sets the winners apart from the losers is the ability to summon up pinpoint mental concentration on the working muscle(s) during every set of an all-out workout. My own level of concentration is so intense and complete that I don't even feel the bar in my hands or across my shoulders as I do a set. I'm only aware of the powerful contraction and smooth extension of the muscle(s) that I'm training.

Here are some examples of improper and proper mental concentration with the lat machine Behind-Neck Pulldown—one of the best movements for bringing out the latissimus dorsi, particularly the upper section of this wedge-shaped back muscle complex. When you aren't concentrating correctly, you will tend to focus on the secondary stress that Behind-Neck Pulldowns place on the rear delts, biceps, brachialis, and forearm flexor muscles, rather than on the primary effect they have on the lats. More often than not, your grip will fail and cause you to stop the set long before your lats have been completely stimulated. Or, your biceps will hurt so much that you will forget all about your lats.

When I'm concentrating on a set of Pulldowns, I use grip-reinforcing straps so that I don't have to give an instant's though to my grip on the lat bar. Then I choose a training weight that isn't so heavy that I'm forced to use heavy body momentum to complete a repetition. I take my grip on the bar, sit on the lat machine seat, firmly wedge my knees behind the restraint bar, and fully straighten my arms.

On a perfectly concentrated Pulldown rep behind the neck, I focus all my attention on my lat muscles on each side strongly contracting as the bar comes downwards lightly touching my traps at the back of my neck. I pause a slow count in this position to be certain that I've achieved total contraction in my lats. Then I focus on the latissimus dorsi muscles extending completely to a stretched position at the end of the rep, when my arms are again held perfectly straight.

Of course, I have practiced Behind-Neck Pulldowns—to say nothing of a couple hundred

other bodybuilding movements—so frequently over such a long period of time that I don't need to worry about maintaining perfect form as I concentrate on each rep. I automatically keep my back arched and elbows held back while I pull almost solely with my lats. Naturally, it takes time to develop this mastery of exercise form and workout concentration.

Since a set performed with 50 percent concentration is only about 5 percent as effective as one performed with 100 percent concentration, you must learn to concentrate well during your workouts. The first step towards mastering workout concentration is to identify which muscles are stressed by certain basic exercises. This can be easily determined by carefully reading the exercise descriptions in bodybuilding books, as well as in the bodybuilding magazine articles dealing with techniques for building various body parts.

Each time you do an exercise, stand in front of a mirror and observe the working muscles in action. As you learn where you should be feeling a particular movement, *feel* it there. Concentrate on those working muscles contracting and extending, never allowing anything to distract you.

At first, your attention will wander. But with time, you will gradually improve your level of workout concentration. This is something you have to work on almost constantly. Every time you notice that your mind has skipped off to another thought, you need to consciously bring it back to the working muscles.

If I ever notice myself losing concentration during a workout, I give myself a little pep talk about how none of my competitors are blowing *their* concentration. After this, the flood that floated Noah's Ark couldn't distract me, and I end up getting a sensational workout.

INSPIRATION AND ENTHUSIASM

Consistent, heavy, all-out bodybuilding workouts—the only type I know of that consistently builds great physiques—require a great deal of personal dedication as well as enthusiasm for the entire bodybuilding process, but particularly for the pumping iron part. While most of us can stay dedicated and motivated to succeed as bodybuilders, almost everyone experiences a day here and there when enthusiasm for workouts seems to have gone out with the tide. In a very real sense, the degree of success you achieve in overcoming low levels of enthusiasm are almost directly proportionate with competitive success.

In my considerable experience training aspiring competitive bodybuilders—men as well as women—I've found that workout enthusiasm is a direct result of how inspired someone is to succeed at the sport. I'm not referring to the average gym rat here, but to my fellow fanatics who not only want to win local, regional, and national physique titles, but also pro bodybuilding championships.

Once you've dedicated yourself to becoming a successful competitor, you'll find that your greatest source of inspiration will be reading bodybuilding magazines. In them, you can read inspiring stories about normal people like you who have become outstanding bodybuilding competitors. And once you're in the "outstanding" class yourself, much of your inspiration will come from reading about and seeing the photos of your fellow competitors.

I strongly recommend buying all of your favorite muscle mags each month and saving them for both future reference and inspiration. There is also a ton of bodybuilding books on the market that can inform and inspire you, as well. Some champs have even published their own specialized training courses. All of these publications have a place in your library for both educational and inspirational purposes.

In the last few years, bodybuilding video tapes have become widely available. They can be training oriented, show past competitions, or highlight the personality of one bodybuilding superstar or another. If you have a VCR—as many people do these days—videos can be tremendously inspirational.

In bringing this section to a close, let me give you my personal formula for getting in an awesome workout when my enthusiasm, for

Self-confidence is essential for a winner.

whatever reasons, has reached a low ebb. I brew up a couple of cups of coffee or tea, grab 10 to 15 back issues of various bodybuilding magazines, and sit down at my kitchen table. As I drink my coffee or tea, I leaf through the mags, paying special attention to those photos of women against whom I'll be competing at the next Ms. Olympia. (If you're competing at a lower level, photos of almost any higher-level champion will have the same effect on you.) A cup or two and five to 10 magazines later, I usually can't wait to get to the gym.

SELF-CONFIDENCE

There is no doubt that self-confidence *shows* onstage; when a competitor has it, she almost glows with a celestial light. Self-confidence permeates the body language of a winner, just as the lack of it is immediately apparent in the body language of a loser. So, it would behoove you to bank away as much self-confidence as possible before your next show. It will bring you many more golden trophies than you'd win as a shrinking violet.

The first step in developing self-confidence is to work on the positive-thinking techniques discussed earlier in this chapter. In addition, do everything possible to continue making steady improvements in your physique, no matter how slowly the gains come. Making these steady improvements is a great confidence-builder.

Once you have gained some solid self-confidence, keep it high by entering just those competitions equal to your present level of development. After winning a local novice show, nothing will deflate your confidence quite like going too far over your head and placing last at an open regional competition.

In terms of self-confidence, you'll do a lot better if you compete at the lowest available level until you win a first-place trophy. Then move up a level—and compete there until you, again, strike gold. It's like climbing a ladder; you move successfully upwards one step at a time—with your self-confidence also increasing a step at a time—until you are one of the best in the sport. Perhaps your level of development and self-confidence will reach such heights that you'll win an IFBB Pro Championship or even Ms. Olympia!

MENTAL VISUALIZATION DRILLS

Our mind can be viewed as having two components—one conscious, the other subconscious. Briefly, the conscious mind makes those mental decisions that we are aware of when we're making them. However, the conscious mind is not always logical in its decisions, often making them more as a result of emotional considerations. In short, the conscious mind can be rather capricious and undependable.

In contrast, the subconscious mind—although we are largely unaware of its workings—is almost totally logical and unemotional. It constantly receives data from the environment, and uses this information to make those decisions that we regard as hunches or instinctive reactions.

The subconscious mind plays a very important role in a bodybuilder's success formula, because it can actually be programmed to make sound bodybuilding decisions, similar to the way a computer is programmed. You can think of your subconscious as an organic computer, which can be effectively used to further your bodybuilding aims.

Psychologists have long recognized a psychological construct called "self-actualization." In self-actualization, someone may daydream, say, of becoming a famous athlete, fabulous dancer, virtuoso pianist, or pioneering surgeon. Daydreams, like this—when done on a near-daily basis—gradually program the subconscious mind to make decisions that will lead to actualization of the dream vocation.

By using the visualization process, you can program your subconscious mind; you can actualize yourself as a top competitive bodybuilder.

Optimally, you should practice visualization with all five of your senses—sight, hearing, touch, taste, and smell. Relatively few people actually use visualization in more than just the imagined sense of sight. But psychological re-

Taking a breather between sets (1986).

search has proven that visualization becomes progressively more effective with each new sense injected into the visualized image.

Visualization should be done as frequently as possible. It is most effectively practiced in a dark, quiet place at a time when you can be sure not to be interrupted or distracted for at least 15 minutes. Bedtime is usually best for practising visualization, and your benefits will be even greater if you fall asleep with your visualized image still in your mind!

Begin the visualization process by first fully relaxing your body. Lie on your back in bed with one pillow under your knees and another beneath your head and neck. Your legs should be slightly parted, and your toes pointed outward at about a 45° angle. Your arms should be down at your sides, 3 or 4 inches from your torso on each side. Close your eyes, and keep them closed throughout your visualization session.

Once you are in this comfortable position, begin to relax your body, one part at a time. This is done by first tensing your left foot and ankle for 15 to 20 seconds, and then fully relaxing those tensed muscles. Repeat this with the right foot and ankle. Gradually work upwards to relax both calves, both hamstrings, both buttocks, both quads, the lower back, the middle back, the traps, the abs, the pectorals on each side, the delts on each side, the biceps on each side, the triceps on each side, the forearms on each side, and the hands on each side. Finish off by relaxing all of your neck muscles and the facial muscles. This relaxation process will probably take 20 to 30 minutes at first; but within a few weeks of daily visualization practice, you will easily get it down to as few as 5 to 7 minutes.

Once you are completely relaxed, begin to work up a visual image of how you would like your physique to appear one year from now. With your mind's eye, see every new ounce of muscle as it bulges around deepened cuts, all of the myriad striations across each major muscle mass, and the thick tracery of vascularity all over your new muscles. Let yourself enjoy this image without embarrassment. The more vivid the visual image is and the more fully you enjoy it, the more quickly and deeply it will be implanted in your subconscious mind.

Let's add the sense of touch to your visual image. Imagine yourself posing all of this perfectly developed new muscle at a show a year from now. As you flow easily from one pose to the next, imagine the feel of those new muscles showing through tissue-paper-thin skin. Feel how they are bigger and harder than they've ever been before.

You can include the senses of smell and hearing into this same visualized posing routine. The scent of the oil you use to highlight all of that new musculature has a distinctive character; it's something you'll always remember once you've been in a show. You can also imagine smelling the odor of honest sweat. And you can hear the crowd roar and applaud your efforts at the prejudging and as you surge powerfully and gracefully through your free-posing routine at the evening show. You *can* hear it, can't you? When you are able to include touching, smelling, and hearing in a visualized image, it's an incredible feeling—you'll want to work to achieve it time after time.

The visualized sense of taste, although a bit boring, also plays a role. For instance, imagine that dry, broiled piece of fish and dry baked potato you will be eating for your fifth meal of the day a week before your show. Get that fifth imagined sense into your visualization practice, and you'll be on your way to the Olympia.

MIND POWER

Never underestimate the power of your mind in turning yourself into a champion bodybuilder. Diet and training are of equal importance in the off-season, with diet rising in importance close to a competition. But all of the training and diet in the world won't give you an ounce of muscle mass if your mind isn't fully into the process. So, *think* your way to the top!

6
CONTEST-LEVEL BODYBUILDING PRINCIPLES

As I became better known as a bodybuilder and began to obtain a lot of bookings for training seminars, I learned that rising young bodybuilders tend to ask a lot of the same questions. Regardless of where I am in this wide world when I give a seminar, one very common question is: "What is the biggest secret to bodybuilding success?" There is no single secret to bodybuilding success. There are 12, which I can identify and which collectively assure success. They are:

- favorable genetics,
- persistence,
- workout consistency,
- self-belief,
- self-confidence,
- intelligence,
- total mental commitment,
- inquisitiveness,
- eliminating fears of either success or failure,
- 100% maintenance of a good bodybuilding diet,
- honest hard work, and
- consistently high training intensity.

The more consistently you work to actualize each of these 12 secrets, the greater your chance of quick success as a bodybuilding competitor.

DESCENDING SETS

In Chapter 3 I discussed cheating and forced reps as ways of increasing intraset training intensity. A third method, used by many contest-level bodybuilders, is descending sets, which are sometimes called stripping or step-bombing. This method enables you to push your working muscles well past the point at which they would normally become so fatigued that they would force you to terminate a set.

In each descending set, you start out with a maximum poundage and a training partner at each end of the barbell—collars off the bar. After you have completed a predetermined number of reps (perhaps, 5 to 8), you will reach a point where you will fail a rep. At that point, your partners will each strip the same amount of weight from their end of the bar (obviously, the amount must be determined prior to your set), and you will continue the set with the decreased poundage. Usually, a second weight drop completes the set, although a few top women I know do three or even four weight drops in a descending set.

Descending sets can be easily performed with dumbbell movements or machine exercises in which a pin is used in the weight stack to determine the poundage. With dumbbells, you can use a technique called "going down the rack," in which you do 6 to 8 reps with one pair of dumbbells, set them back on the rack, and then pick up the next-lightest pair and do as many reps as possible—continuing down the rack with as many as 5 to 8 weight drops. This technique makes it easy for you to do descending sets yourself when you don't have two training partners available to help you. It requires only a rack of dumbbells in graduated weights, as well as plenty of your own go-power!

Using one training partner, you can perform your descending sets on machines with selectorized weight stacks. Just get into the machine, with the pin set far enough down the stack to give you a weight that would cause you to fail at between 5 and 8 reps. Then, if you pause for a second or two, your partner can quickly move the selector pin one plate or more up the stack, almost instantly reducing the poundage. Again, a couple of weight drops will do the trick.

Descending sets are a *very* intense way to train, and they will give you great results in increasing muscle mass. However, because descending sets are so intense, you should break into them very carefully. At first, you should try only one descending set, per body part, on the final set of your first basic movement for that muscle complex. Then increase the number you do for each body part very gradually, always keeping on the lookout for any signs that you are pushing too hard and risking overtraining.

QUALITY TRAINING

In general, there are four ways to increase the overload you place on your working muscles.

Selectorized weight stacks make it particularly easy to change poundages. As quick as a wink, you can select a different weight by simply moving the selector pin upwards or downwards.

Changing weights on a selectorized weight stack.

They are:
- increase the amount of weight being used for a specific number of repetitions;
- increase the number of reps you are doing with a particular weight;
- increase the total number of sets done with a particular weight for a specific number of reps; and
- continue to do the same number of sets and reps with the same weight in a movement, but gradually reduce the length of rest intervals between sets.

Bodybuilders relatively new to the sport often increase resistance by combining the first three of these methods. They gradually increase the number of total sets performed for each muscle group, being certain that they don't go so high in total sets that they slip over into an overtrained condition. They also combine increasing reps with increasing poundages, usually increasing reps—say, from 8 up to 12—and then dropping the reps back to 8 once 12 have been accomplished, while concurrently increasing the weight. They continue this process almost *ad infinitum*.

In contrast, contest-level bodybuilders—when in a peaking cycle—tend to forget all about increasing their poundages and reps in such a systematic manner. Instead, they augment both resistance and intensity by progressively reducing their rest intervals from an average of 60 to 90 seconds (perhaps up to 2 minutes between sets of exercises for the largest muscle groups) down to as few as 15 seconds.

Incidentally, when peaking, most champion bodybuilders also increase both total sets for each muscle group and reps per set as ways of further hardening up. Also, a calorie-restricted or carbohydrate-restricted diet has a significant effect on the degree of muscularity a bodybuilder displays onstage at a competition.

Rest intervals must be reduced systematically—say, by about 5 or 10 seconds per week. Starting out at 90-second rest intervals at the beginning of your peaking cycle, you could be down to 30 seconds in six convenient weekly reductions of 5 seconds each.

Due to a strict precontest diet and more speedy workouts, you will inevitably find that your training poundages must be progressively dropped. Most bodybuilders find that they lose 30 to 50 percent on their exercise weights over the length of a peaking cycle. But as long as you constantly fight to keep your poundages up—regardless of how difficult this is—you will receive the benefits of quality training, even with the reduced poundages.

Some bodybuilders do *not* use the quality-training technique as a competition approaches. Instead, they try to gradually increase workout poundages throughout their peaking cycle, while taking normal off-season rest breaks between sets. Proponents of this practice believe that it encourages peak muscle mass *with* sharp muscularity. I suggest giving both methods an off-season trial to determine which one works best for you. But don't try them prior to a show, unless you're merely using that competition as a learning experience and don't care about whether or not you win.

PEAK CONTRACTION

Exercise physiologists talk about an "all or nothing" model for muscle contraction. By this, they mean that each muscle cell either contracts completely (all) under a load, or it does not contract at all (nothing). To understand the ramifications of this model as it relates to your advanced bodybuilding efforts, you will need to know something about muscle anatomy.

The smallest unit of a skeletal muscle is a muscle cell, which looks somewhat like an oblong rectangle or a fattened oval. Individual muscle cells are strung end-to-end to form muscle fibres. Large groups of muscle fibres are bundled together to form a skeletal muscle.

In order to lift a weight in a particular bodybuilding exercise, individual muscle cells must contract to shorten the fibres, and hence to shorten the skeletal muscle to move the weight. The heavier the weight—and the shorter the fibre becomes—the greater the number of individual cells that must be contracted.

Bottom position of Squat.

Since, as I just said, the maximum number of cells is contracted when your skeletal muscle is fully shortened (contracted), it makes sense that you should have a maximum poundage placed against that muscle mass when it's in its contracted position. Scientific experiments have demonstrated that you achieve greater muscle stimulation—and consequently greater muscle hypertrophy—when you stress the skeletal muscle maximally when it is in the contracted position. And this is the basis of the peak contraction principle of training.

However, a problem arises, because many free-weight movements do not place a lot of stress on the working muscle when it's completely contracted. Let's use Standing Barbell Curls as an example. The greatest amount of stress occurs when your forearm is parallel with the floor. When your arm is completely bent (the position you're in when the barbell has reached shoulder level), the biceps are contracting with very little force. Indeed, most of the resistance is felt by the deltoids and upper-back muscles.

There are several ways that you can place maximum stress on your biceps when they are fully contracted. One is to do barbell or dumbbell Concentration Curls with your torso held parallel to the floor and your upper arm(s) hanging straight down from your shoulders. In this position, you'll find that you actually have to fight hard to curl the bar up to your shoulders, and you'll have to exert your biceps mightily in order to keep it at the top point of the movement.

A second way to maximally stress your biceps in the fully contracted position is to do Machine Curls. When you use a machine, the cam (pulley arrangement) of the machine automatically keeps the force vector of the weight at a right angle to your forearm throughout the movement, and that in turn keeps stress constantly intense, even at the top of the exercise's range of movement.

Since you should always include peak contraction movements in your body part routines, you should know which exercises provide peak contraction. Here is a list of the best ones for each body part:

Legs—Leg Extensions, Leg Curls, and Pulley/Machine Abductions and Adductions

Calves—virtually all exercises

Lower Back—Hyperextensions, Nautilus Hip and Back Machine

Traps—all types of Shrugs and Upright Rows

Lats—all types of Pulldowns, Chins, and Rows

Delts—all types of Lateral Raises (side, front, bent-over)

Chest—Pec Deck Flyes, Cable Crossovers, and Machine Bench Presses

Biceps—Bent-Over Concentration Curls (barbell/dumbbell) and Machine Curls

Triceps—Nautilus Triceps Extensions and Barbell/Dumbbell Kickbacks

Forearms—Wrist Curls/Reverse Wrist Curls done with the forearms running down a decline bench, hands hanging off the lower edge

Abdominals—Hanging Leg Raises, all types of Crunches

CONTINUOUS TENSION

Every degree of additional intensity you can place on your skeletal muscles during a peaking cycle will bring you to a higher peak. The continuous tension technique will add quite a bit of intensity to a set, and it's one of the best ways of etching the maximum number of striations across each major muscle mass. Using continuous tensions, your deltoids will become so ripped up, for example, that you'll look like you had a painful encounter with a jungle cat.

Many bodybuilders make the mistake of allowing momentum to help move a weight upwards. They do the rep so quickly that the bar literally flies up on its own, robbing the muscles of much of the stress they should be feeling—stress that should be improving their muscular development. Simply by slowing the movement down a little, you will reduce momentum and add stress to your working muscles—and this is the first part of continuous tension.

The second part is tensing the muscles throughout the full positive and negative range

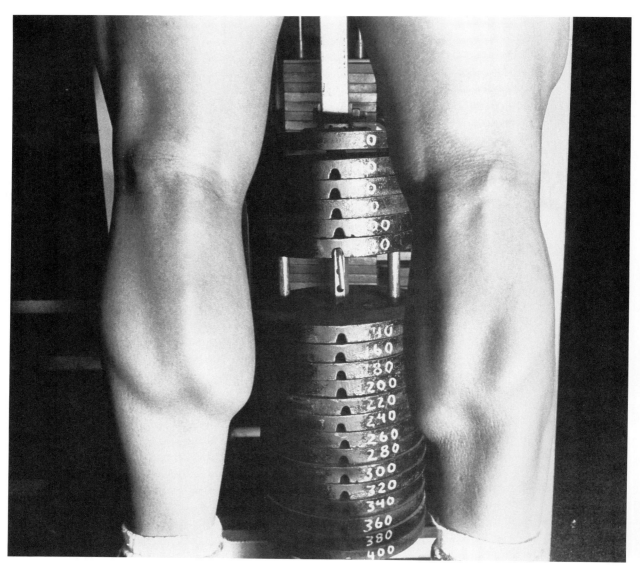

Standing Calf Raise (1986).

of each repetition so that they are forced to *feel* the weight over every inch of its rise and fall. By contracting antagonistic muscle groups (such as triceps when you're working biceps), you can add even more quality to the repetition. The bar grinds upwards and downwards each rep, and you really feel the resistance.

When you slow down a movement and add a great deal of muscle tension, you automatically limit the amount of weight you can use for each set. But this shouldn't worry you, as long as you are using an amount that is the relative maximum possible for that set. Continuous tension adds intensity to such an extent that a reduction in training weights has virtually no consequence.

TRISETS AND GIANT SETS

I began a discussion of compounded exercises in Chapter 3 with an explanation of how to use supersets, or compounds of two movements. But there are two more steps up the ladder of intensity when it comes to compounding exercises for one muscle group or more—trisets and giant sets.

Trisets are compounds of three exercises, usually for one complex muscle group—such as the back, chest, delts, or legs. These are several examples of trisets:

DELTOIDS
Standing Barbell Presses (anterior head)
Dumbbell Side Laterals (medial head)
Cable Bent Laterals (posterior head)

CHEST
Incline Dumbbell Presses (upper pecs)
Pec Deck Flyes (inner-middle pecs)
Decline Flyes (lower-outer pecs)

BACK
Seated Pulley Rows (lat thickness)
Front Machine Pulldowns (lat width)
Stiff-Arm Pulldowns (lat/upper back details)

LEGS
Angled Leg Presses (quadriceps mass)
Leg Curls (biceps femoris development)
Leg Extensions (quadriceps detail/shape)

Leg Extensions (1986).
Continuous tension adds intensity.

A quick analysis of the four routines just presented will show you that trisets allow you to train multifaceted muscles from three different angles at once. As such, they are not only a significant step upwards in intensity from supersets, but they are also a big step up in developmental effect. They work particularly well when you are in a peaking phase prior to competition.

Giant sets are groupings of 4 to 6 movements for either a single, very complex muscle group, or two antagonistic body parts. Going up the intensity ladder, 4-movement giant sets for antagonistic muscle groups are the least intense type, followed in upwards-intensity order by 4 movement giant sets for a single muscle complex, 5-movement giant sets for antagonistic groups, 5-movement giant sets for a single muscle complex, 6-movement giant sets for antagonistic groups, and 6-movement giant sets for antagonistic groups, and 6-movement giant sets for a single, ultracomplex body part.

Each step up the foregoing ladder of intensity for compound sets requires a much greater expenditure of energy than the lower rung. As a result, you should be careful to break in slowly and gradually when moving up from one intensity level to the next.

The following are examples of all six of the aforementioned types of giant sets:

FOUR EXERCISES (BICEPS + TRICEPS)
Standing Barbell Curls
Lying Barbell Triceps Extensions
Barbell Concentration Curls
Pulley Push-Downs

FOUR EXERCISES (BACK ONLY)
Chins Behind Neck (lat width)
Hyperextensions (lower back)
Barbell Bent Rows (lat thickness)
Rotating Dumbbell Shrugs (trapezius)

FIVE EXERCISES (BACK + CHEST)
Front Lat Machine Pulldowns
Incline Dumbbell Presses
T-Bar Rows
Bench Presses to Neck
Cross-Bench Pullovers

FIVE EXERCISES (LEGS ONLY)
Squats
Lying Leg Curls
Sissy Squats
Stiff-Legged Deadlifts
Leg Extensions

SIX EXERCISES (BICEPS + TRICEPS)
Seated Alternate Dumbbell Curls
Lying Barbell Triceps Extensions
Machine Curls
Pulley Push-Downs
Standing Wide-Grip Barbell Curls
Dips Between Benches

SIX EXERCISES (BACK ONLY)
Machine Rows
Barbell Shrugs
Pulldowns Behind Neck
Hyperextensions
Front Lat Machine Pulldowns
Cross-Bench Pullovers

Pulley Push-Downs — start.

Pulley Push-Downs — finish.

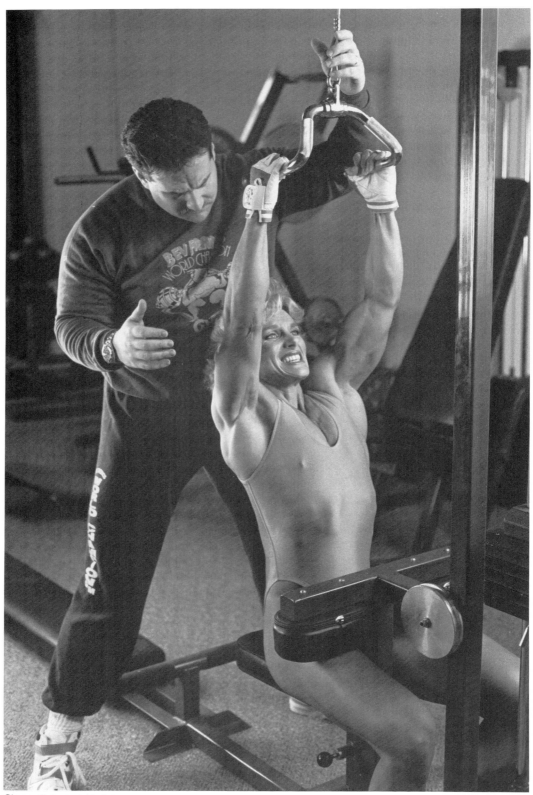
Close-Grip Lat Pulldowns — start.

Close-Grip Lat Pulldowns — finish.

A weightlifting belt is often used when performing heavy squats, back exercises, and overhead lifts. It adds stability to the midsection, protecting both the abdomen and lower back from injury.

BELTS AND WRAPS

During the process of preparing for and winning six consecutive World Powerlifting Championships (1980 through 1985, in the 165- and 181-pounds weight classes), I learned a lot about using weightlifting belts and body wraps to assist me in lifting heavy weights. By wearing a very tight "supersuit," a tightly fastened lifting belt, and tight knee wraps, a high-level female powerlifter can add 30 to 60 pounds to her best Squat.

As I said in Chapter 2, however, bodybuilders should be "feelers" rather than "lifters." To some extent, using heavy weights is important to bodybuilders, because the more weight you use with strict form in a particular movement, the larger and more detailed will be the muscles that move that weight. But bodybuilders make gains in muscle mass and quality more from high-intensity training methods than from lifting exceptionally heavy poundages in their workouts. Therefore, as a bodybuilder, you should avoid using supersuits entirely, and use belts and wraps only to protect yourself from injury, not to help you lift more.

The only time a weightlifting belt is essential is when you do various types of Squats, since it protects both the lower back and abdomen during the movement. Otherwise, it's best to limit belt use to protecting prior or existing injuries to the midsection. Even then, it will only be needed when you do Deadlifts, heavy Bent-Over Rows, and overhead pressing exercises.

Body wraps come in two types, neophrene rubber bands or elastic fabric bandages. Rubber wraps give a minimum of support, but retain damp body heat over an injured area, which can be quite therapeutic. These wraps can be used on the knees or elbows, or around the waist (when your lower back is hurting). They are widely available in sporting goods shops, as well as by mail order through advertisements in various bodybuilding magazines.

In contrast to the rubber variety, fabric wraps don't retain heat, but do provide considerable support to an injured joint. Most frequently, bodybuilders use them wrapped around their knees when doing heavy Squats and/or Leg Presses. But they can also be utilized to protect injured elbows, wrists, or ankles. As with weightlifting belts, unless you are trying to protect an old injury site, don't grow dependent on wraps. Your muscles—not the belts or wraps—should be lifting the weights.

INSTINCTIVE TRAINING ABILITY

Experienced bodybuilders ultimately become so conscious of biofeedback signals from their bodies that they develop an instinct—or intuition—for exactly which exercise and dietary variables build the most muscle. The more quickly you learn how to monitor and interpret the information your body is sending back to your mind, the faster will be your ultimate progress in the sport.

What do I mean by biofeedback signals? Two of the most easily noticed signals are muscle pump and muscle soreness. A good pump, that pleasant and tightly congested feeling in your muscles, is a certain indication that the workout you just completed is working for you. Next-day muscle soreness is an equally certain signal that the previous day's workout hit your muscles more intensely than under normal circumstances.

There are many other biofeedback signals that you should be monitoring, including:

- fatigue levels,
- changes in body fat levels,
- visible changes in the contour of your muscles,
- tactile changes in muscle density,
- increases (or losses) in strength levels,
- relative soreness of joints and/or muscles over a longer term than day-to-day,
- relative ability to relax and/or sleep,
- mental alertness,
- willingness to undertake each workout,
- speed of recovery between workouts,
- how the exercises feel to your muscles,
- intensity of muscle contractions,
- feeling of well-being,
- changes in speed with which you can perform your workout (shorter or longer rest intervals between sets),
- sensations of hunger, and
- sensations within the muscles during your recovery cycle.

Maintaining a detailed training diary is one of the quickest ways to learn precisely how your body responds to various training and dietary stimuli. Be sure to review it at least once a month in order to establish patterns of particularly quick muscle growth.

The foregoing 16 variables—as well as many more that will occur to you as you progress through your bodybuilding career—should be correlated with progress phases. And once you begin to make connections between certain types of biofeedback data and spurts in muscle growth, you will know what to look for in the future. Then it becomes easy to discover whether or not a new training or dietary variable is working for you in as short a period of time as one or two days. Without this training instinct, it would probably take you weeks or even months.

Obviously, it is difficult to notice gains from week to week, unless you keep a comprehensive training diary. Gradual upwards trends in strength levels are a sure indication that you're improving, as are changes in physical appearance—which are two reasons why you should have photos taken of yourself in standard poses every couple of months, and then paste them in your diary. Without a diary, you're guessing; with one, you have concrete data at your fingertips.

There are commercial diaries available in bookstores and gyms, or through mail-order ads in muscle magazines. They have preprinted pages, where you can enter your exercises, weights, sets, reps, and any other information that could eventually help you develop a good training instinct.

Of course, you can also use any type of bound pages or a spiral-bound notebook. Many serious bodybuilders like the type of bound ledger book that can be found in all office supply shops. Confronted with blank pages, you will need to develop some sort of format for your diary entries. At a minimum, you should include the day's date, every exercise you perform, and weights, sets, and reps executed on that movement. Other possible entries would include how much time it took to complete the workout, an assessment of your mental attitude and energy levels before and after each gym session, aerobics you perform, your daily body weight, how much you slept the night before, and any existing injuries you might have on the day of the workout.

With blank pages, you can also include a detailed write-up of what you ate (perhaps with daily summaries of the number of calories as well as grams of protein, carbs, and fat consumed) and which food supplements you took. Be sure to list the amounts of each food and food supplement. Since diet and training are basically of equal importance in the off-season, you should definitely consider making dietary entries. It takes a little time, but is well worth it.

Month after month, year after year, you should make diary entries and keep your diaries in a safe place. But no workout diary in the world is going to do you any good unless you constantly refer back to past weeks, months, and years of training and eating. Constantly reviewing your diary notes is the only way you'll be able to see trends in muscular development, and spot the reasons for them, so that you can duplicate periods of fast gains in the future.

By keeping a training diary, you will be able to develop a good training instinct within a year to a year and a half, versus the four or five years it would probably take if you were just guessing at what you did in a workout, say, a year ago. Once you have reliable training instincts, you will be well on your way to winning a high-level amateur or professional title!

7

PRO-LEVEL BODYBUILDING SECRETS

Let's talk about public relations—that is, your relationship as a bodybuilder to the general public. First off, you have to realize that the average man or woman on the street knows very little about your sport. Frequently, they form many of their opinions about the entire sport based upon encountering only one or two serious bodybuilders. If the bodybuilder they encounter is you, everyone in the sport hopes that you come off as a well-rounded person who happens to also have a great physique, rather than as just one more musclehead.

I believe that there are two places where you have a right to show off your hard-earned muscles—at the beach and at bodybuilding competitions. In all other situations, I personally dress conservatively—often in loose clothing and long-sleeved tops, which reveal very little of my muscular development. One thing that immediately turns off someone outside the sport is to see a puffed-up bodybuilder in a tank top and shorts, lats spread to the hilt, every muscle tensed, strutting along the street.

You'll do a lot more for the sport if you present yourself as a relaxed, intelligent person. No one has to be a musclehead, unless she wants to. Spend some time developing aspects of your personality that have nothing to do with the sport, and try to come across as a well-adjusted, pleasant person. You'll speak well for the sport of bodybuilding if you do.

DOUBLE-SPLIT ROUTINES

Many bodybuilders, myself included, follow a double-split routine prior to a competition. Some even train twice per day year-round. To some novice bodybuilders, this might seem like a lot of trouble to go to—having to change clothes several times a day and take two showers, just so they can do two workouts in the gym each training day. But to an experienced competitive bodybuilder, split routines make a lot of sense.

It has been scientifically established that the body's basal metabolic rate (usually abbreviated as BMR) rises during any type of physical exercise, and it stays at a higher-than-normal level for several hours afterwards. Close to a competition, most bodybuilders train at least two or three times per day (aerobics sessions included), simply to keep the BMR high for a longer period of time each day, and thereby making it easier to burn off excess body fat and achieve a truly ripped-up condition.

By double-splitting, you also shorten the length of each training session. This is an important consideration—particularly when your energy levels are low as a result of a restricted precontest diet. If you do your entire routine in one session, it's highly likely that you will run out of gas long before you have completed your training program, which means you'll give short shrift to the last few exercises in your routine. But with your program divided into two parts, your workouts will be less than half of their normal length, and you will have plenty of time during the middle of the day to rest; and this will allow you to train consistently all-out, rather than dragging through half of your training schedule.

Generally, bodybuilders train for the first time in the morning, (ideally) take a nap in the early afternoon, and then return in the late afternoon or evening to complete the second half of their double-split. Here is an example of how you can divide up your various body parts for a

Onstage at the '88 Ms. Olympia.

double-split; it's a three-on/one-off scheme used by most top bodybuilders:

DAY 1 (AM)
Abdominals
Chest

DAY 1 (PM)
Shoulders
Calves

DAY 2 (AM)
Abdominals
Back

DAY 2 (AM)
Triceps
Forearms

DAY 3 (AM)
Abdominals
Quadriceps

DAY 3 (PM)
Calves
Leg Biceps
Biceps

Notice the pattern of doing one large muscle group and one smaller body part each of the twice-daily training sessions. The manner in which you actually split up your training program is a matter of personal choice—but however you divide things up, try to follow this basic pattern.

ECLECTIC BODYBUILDING

If you are an eclectic bodybuilder, you approach your training, dietary, and mental-approach philosophies from the maximum possible number of angles, leaving no stone unturned in your quest for physical perfection. But eclectic bodybuilding also refers to a specific method of training in which you deliberately choose to attack a particular muscle group from a maximum number of angles.

For the most complete muscular development, you *must*, over a period of years, attack each body part from every possible angle. This means never getting into a rut using the same exercises all the time or staying with a single favorite movement for a particular muscle complex. You can also train eclectically within each body part workout.

In an eclectic muscle-group training session, start out with one basic exercise, pyramiding up from a light poundage to a heavy set of 5 or 6 reps within about 5 total sets. This will ensure that you're sufficiently warmed up to avoid any injuries, as you move from one exercise to the next, doing only one or 2 sets per movement.

Consider that basic exercise—Barbell Incline Presses for the chest, for example—as your warm-up. The remainder of your workout should consist of performing almost every exercise you can think of for a particular area. Then, being sure not to exceed about 15 total sets for a body part, use a moderately heavy weight on each movement and do one set of 8 to 10 reps of every exercise.

If you can't include every movement you know for your chest, back, legs, or whatever, be sure to do those that remain the next time you work the same muscle group. In this manner, you'll get around to almost all of the appropriate exercises available to you over a cycle of two or three training sessions.

You can get extremely sore muscles if you attempt to do an entire eclectic workout the first time you follow that training principle. This occurs because you are placing a much greater-than-normal degree of stress on a muscle group, and from the widest possible number of angles. Therefore, you should be sure to break slowly into the full routine you've planned for yourself.

ISO-TENSION

Over the past couple of decades, bodybuilders discovered that there was a correlation between the amount of posing they did during a precontest cycle and the ultimate degree of muscularity they achieved. Simply put, the more they posed, the harder they appeared onstage competing.

Today, competitive bodybuilders use iso-tension, or deliberate and intense flexions of each muscle group, to add the finishing touches to their muscularity before a contest. This technique consists of doing repetitive flexes lasting about 8 to 10 seconds each, followed by a short rest interval of about 10 seconds, and then another series of flexes. Up to 50 of these rep flexes can be done daily for each muscle group.

It's best to do your iso-tension work in front of a mirror so that you can monitor the degree of muscularity you are bringing out with each bout of tension. And you should be sure to flex each individual skeletal muscle in a wide variety of positions, or poses. By monitoring your phy-

Manual strengthening exercises for the neck.

sique in the mirror this way, you'll learn little tricks that will bring out additional tiny details within each muscle group while you're posing.

Iso-tension work is also essential in your preparation for the prejudging at a major competition. It's very fatiguing to do many comparison poses at a show, and you'd end up shaking like a leaf after only a few comparisons if you didn't practice holding your compulsory poses for long periods of time. Up to one minute in each pose wouldn't be excessive. Doing minute-long poses in practice is nothing in comparison to long-lasting iso-tension work.

POSING

There are three primary judging rounds of posing, and a special posedown, and each requires a different style of physique presentation. The order of the judging rounds is occasionally changed, but currently they are as follows:

Round One—Compulsory poses (front double-biceps, side chest, back double-biceps, side triceps, and front abdominal-and-thigh pose with hands held behind the head or neck).

A comparison of Most Muscular poses at the '88 Ms. Olympia between myself and Cory Everson.

Round Two—What's often called the "symmetry round," this consists of presenting your physique in a semirelaxed stance with arms down at the sides and feet close together, showing the front, one side, the back, and the other side of your physique in order.

Round Three—Free posing to your own musical selection.

Posedown—An exciting, free-flowing woman-to-woman confrontation, in which you try for a final few, crucial points by showing off your physique in your best individualized poses.

In the following detailed discussion of these four rounds of posing, you will learn how you can improve your own physical presentation skills. Master posing, and you're well on your way to winning a title.

Round One

While the competition rules state which five poses must be performed in the compulsories round, each pose is definitely open to individual interpretation. To see for yourself how many variations exist of each mandatory pose, try cutting out photos of every front double-biceps pose you spot within the pages of various bodybuilding magazines. Then line up the photos side by side across your living room floor, and take note of how each woman champion does the pose somewhat differently in order to show off her unique physical characteristics.

The only way to devise your own interpretation of the various compulsory poses is to spend plenty of time in front of the mirror working on them. With subtle shifts of foot, leg, hand, arm, torso, hip and head positions, you can gradually evolve five poses that will show your physique off to its best advantage.

It may take many months to discover your best posing positions, so don't wait around until the last possible minute to start practising them. Initiate the process at least 6 to 8 months before your first show, and then continue to work on the five poses throughout your competitive body-

At the prejudging for the '88 Ms. Olympia, Ellen van Maris from Holland and I compare abdominal development in one of the five standardized mandatory poses. In the back lineup, from left to right, are Cathey Palyo (USA) and Janice Ragain (USA).

building career. There's always room for improvement, regardless of how well you feel you have a particular pose mastered.

The performance tips for the five poses that follow should help you with this process.

Front Double-Biceps Pose: On all poses I coach, athletes start from the floor and work upwards, so let's think about setting your feet in the correct position. But what is the correct position? This can vary from holding your feet almost together, which is the method used by Cory Everson (five-times Ms. Olympia) to one in which your feet are spread outward as wide as shoulder width or slightly more. The width between your feet will affect how well you show off your calf and thigh development, so experiment with every possible positioning. You also need to think about whether you want your feet to face straight forward, be out to the sides at various angles, or assume a combination of these positions.

While you will undoubtedly be able to flex your calves most completely with your toes pointed maximally, most bodybuilders avoid that extreme, since it balls the calf up too much and makes it appear short-looking. Because calf shape and mass are influenced by the degree of ankle flexion, you need to experiment with various ankle flexion angles. You can even bring out your calves to an amazing degree with your feet flat on the floor, if you practice it enough.

You'll also be able to flex your quads to the max with your legs straight, but very few top bodybuilders do front leg poses with the knees locked. Instead, you can attain a better quad sweep and still display a great deal of muscularity by unlocking your knees and bending each leg a little; the degree of bend usually varies from one leg to the other.

For optimum torso flare upwards from your waist, do this pose with the front of your torso facing directly towards the judges. With practice, you'll learn the best way to flare out your lats with your arms up in the pose. Usually, this requires a good degree of scapula flexibility on each side; as you spread out your scapulae, the lats follow.

On a front double-bi, you can either use a stomach vacuum or hold a position in which your abs are tensed to bring out each row of muscle in your rectus abdominis. Experiment with each position, or perhaps start out the pose with a vacuum and then contract down into a crunched abs position halfway through the comparison. In general, you'll get better lat sweep with a vacuum, and more total frontal muscularity with the tensed abs.

When you flex your arms, your upper arms should be no lower than a position parallel with the floor. The elbows can be lifted upwards a bit higher than that if it makes your arm position appear more esthetic and effective. The degree of arm flexion can also vary widely, from one at about a 90° angle to one in which your arms are almost completely folded up. You can achieve different looks to your biceps peak by either supinating or pronating your hand a little more than usual.

Side Chest Pose: The foot position in this pose is about the same for everyone. Your feet should be set parallel, with your side facing towards the judges. Your feet can vary from about 3 to 8 inches apart. Keeping the foot away from the judges flat on the floor, rise up on the other toe, while simultaneously bending your leg about 20°. Tense both calves in this position.

You can make the sides of your legs appear more impressive by completely tensing all of your upper-leg muscles. You can make your hamstrings look thicker by pulling the knee on the side of the judges across the midline of your body and towards the back of the stage.

A side-chest pose can be done with either a vacuum or tensed abs, but the vacuum variation is more popular. With your torso erect, bend the arm towards the judges at about a 90° angle, palm facing either directly upwards or more towards the midline of your body. The hand position primarily affects the appearance of your forearm in this pose. Reach across your abdomen with your free hand and either clasp hands or grasp the wrist of your arm towards the judges; your grasping hand should be facing towards the floor. Pull the judges' side shoulder a bit back, the other one a bit forward. Tense all of the chest, shoulder, and arm muscles, pressing your flexed arm against your side to flatten it out and make it appear a bit thicker. Experiment with various degrees of arm bend and hand rotation. Look towards the judges when you have the pose completely composed.

Back Double-Biceps Pose: The rules for this pose dictate that one leg must be extended to the rear and the calf on that leg flexed by going up on your toes. Choose your best leg for this, and play around with various degrees of ankle flexion for best calf display. Grip the stage floor with the toes of your other foot to help bring out some cuts in that calf. Experiment with various widths of foot placement for best lower- and upper-leg display. Be sure your hamstrings on both legs are completely flexed to bring out every possible detail in that area. Also, tense your buttocks in order to eliminate any shaking in that area as you execute the pose.

You'll get the most out of your back double-bi if you arch your back somewhat as you do the pose. And by tensing your abdominal muscles hard, you can bring out every tiny detail of lower-back muscularity; this happens automatically. At the same time, you can automatically bring out greater detail in your traps by turning your head hard to one side or the other, as if you are looking over at your flexed biceps on that side.

When you bring your arms up into the double-biceps pose position, you should experiment with various types of arm bend and hand supination/pronation, as was described for the front variation of the pose. You can bring out greater contour and detail in your delts if you forcefully rotate your upper-arm bones in their sockets so that your hands travel 3 or 4 inches directly to the rear as you have your arms flexed. Be certain that your arms and delts are fully tensed throughout the pose.

By experimenting with varieties of shoulder blade spread—from having them pushed hard together (which brings out greater mid-back muscularity) to having them completely spread (which adds width to the lats)—you can gradually determine the correct position for best mid-back presentation. Obviously, you'll need to set up two mirrors in your posing area in order to gain a direct view of your dorsal area as you do your various back poses, including the back double-biceps shot.

Side Triceps Pose: Traditionally, this pose is done with the leg towards the judges extended to the rear. So, balance yourself with your front foot about 6 inches more towards the back of the stage than your rear foot, and about 12 to 15 inches ahead of it. Grip the floor with the toes of the foot extended forward, and extend the ankle of the rear foot, going up on your toes. Flex both calf muscles, as well as all of your upper-leg muscles.

Reach behind your back with the hand away from the judging panel and grasp the wrist of the hand facing towards the judges. Straighten the arm towards the judges to allow complete tension of your triceps. (As an alternative, you can experiment with various slight degrees of bend in that arm in order to better display your triceps on that arm.) Simultaneously pull backwards with the hand grasping the display arm and pull forward with your deltoid and pectoral muscles; this is a movement that brings out striations in both the shoulder and chest muscles. Be sure to press your display arm against your torso to make it appear a little thicker than it actually is.

There are a few other little tricks that you can try in order to improve this pose. By turning your head forcefully to bring your face towards the judges, you can bring out all of the muscles on your neck. By using a vacuum to suck in your abs, you can make your chest, arm, and shoulder appear exaggeratedly large. And by leaning slightly forward at the waist, you can achieve subtle variations that can also improve the pose. The more little, unique touches you can add to a pose, the better it will suit your unique body.

Front Abdominal-and-Thigh Pose: The rules for this particular pose, as is the case with the back double-biceps shot, dictate that one leg be extended forward and its quad and calf muscles tensed for optimum display. So, start by setting the foot of your best leg forward 8 to 12 inches ahead and slightly out to the side from the foot set firmly on the floor. Extend your foot

sufficiently to allow optimum calf display. Then play with various degrees of leg bend to allow the best possible display of your quadriceps. You'll find that you can bring out your sartorius and inner-thigh muscularity better with a bent leg, and your front and outer quads best with your leg held fairly straight, if not actually straight. For a special effect, you can switch back and forth between the two extremes.

The rules dictate holding both hands behind your head and/or neck as you do this pose, so don't practice it in any other manner. With your arms up and hands behind your neck, you can still flex your biceps intensely and bring out roundness that wouldn't be there if you didn't bother to tense your arms. And by pulling downwards with your hands against your neck, you can improve contour and detail in your lats and pectoral muscles, both of which must also be tensed completely.

Let's work on the abdominal display now. First off, you'll get a lot more out of it if you forcefully blow out all of your air as you go into the pose. If you were judging a competition—or perhaps sitting in the front row—you'd hear every athlete forcefully exhale as she goes into this pose. Then suck in your lower abs and bear down hard to bring out every possible ridge of front-ab muscularity. This techniques takes plenty of practice, to say nothing of lots of abdominal work, to perfect; so work on it consistently, preferably several hours after a meal, when your stomach is relatively empty and you can do the pose with peak efficiency. By turning your torso slightly and bending to the side a bit, you can also bring out your intercostals and obliques. So, shift back and forth between the two abdominal positions once you have mastered each type of display.

For all of your compulsory poses, it's a good idea to rotate your torso slightly to each side so that the judges at both extreme ends of the panel will be able to see you from your best angle. This is sort of an advanced-level skill, one that's not often seen at the lower levels of the sport; so, you can surprise a few people if you do it during your course of physical display at an early-level competition.

Round Two

The symmetry-round stances will undoubtedly be boring for most bodybuilders to practice. So, to keep from missing out on working them altogether, perhaps you should start off each posing practice session with these four semirelaxed facing stances. Certainly, they should be practiced for the same amount of time each session as the other two rounds, since they count for the same number of points on your final score.

Mastering optimum display in these four stances requires plenty of time in front of a mirror, making minute adjustments in the width of your foot placement and the way you hold your legs, torso, arms, hands, and head. Just remember that you don't have to stand perfectly relaxed, but rather partially tensed. Your legs should be tensed almost completely—and your abdominals should be partially flexed, if you look better with them that way.

Unlike the case with the mandatory poses, it's difficult for me to give you specific performance techniques for the four stances used in this judging round. But if you keep at it long enough, you'll gradually work these out for yourself, until you can look your best with your arms down at your sides and your feet held relatively close together.

Round Three

A lot of bodybuilders make the same mistake when choosing shots for the free-posing round—they become too conscious of doing just front shots, or doing poses almost exclusively from one side or the other. What the judges are looking for in this round is a balanced presentation, which includes a fair share of back poses and an almost equal number done from each side.

At the same time, however, the free-posing round does allow you to choose poses that display your strong points to the maximum while camouflaging or minimizing your weaker areas. So, be sure to select only those poses that allow you to appear at your best. The rules of posing-round three allow this, so go for it!

Most bodybuilders naturally begin to practice various poses in front of a mirror as soon as

they start to show a little bit of muscular development, so I probably needn't coach readers on this point. But if you haven't begun this process, it starts with looking for poses that appeal to you in various bodybuilding magazines, and then trying them out in front of the mirror. Obviously, you won't do each pose exactly the way you see it depicted in a magazine, since you'll have to make adjustments to accommodate your unique type of development. These are the same adjustments already discussed for the mandatory poses—adjustments that make your physique appear at its best.

With plenty of time in front of the mirror and a lot of experimentation, you'll eventually come up with unique individual shots that no one has ever done before. These poses—or perhaps only a single shot—will become your trademark, stamping you as a unique, well-recognized competitor. When other athletes begin to use "your" pose, they'll probably call it the "So-and-So pose"—So-and-So being your last name. Then, you will have achieved a small degree of immortality in the sport, and a well-deserved reputation as an innovative poser.

You will be doing your free-posing program to your own choice of music, so give it plenty of thought. Pick a selection that either inspires you or uniquely reflects your personality. At the professional level, there is no limit to the amount of time you can spend free-posing, but amateurs are currently restricted to 60 seconds onstage. So, if you're an amateur, be certain that your musical selection has been professionally recorded and limited to that length of time.

Once you have selected your poses for the free-posing round, you'll need to start stringing them together with suitable transitions. These transitions can be flashy, arty, or merely workmanlike, but they need to be there—and they need to be carried out at least 50 percent of full flexion, settling into a 100 percent flex at each new stop, each successive pose.

There are several ways that you can develop appropriate transitions between poses. If you have a dance or gymnastics background, it will be easy for you to come up with excellent transitional moves between poses. If you have no dance background, you can still use dance techniques, which are very popular in women's competitions, by employing a choreographer. Either ask around the gym for recommendations, or call various dance studios in the yellow pages to find a choreographer adventurous enough to work with you. This costs a little bit of money, but it's well spent if it allows you to look more professional and fully prepared onstage.

If you don't have access to a choreographer or posing coach, I strongly suggest that you purchase several videotapes of competitions, and observe them carefully for moves that you can use in your own routine. These tapes are widely advertised in bodybuilding magazines, and they aren't that expensive. In this age of VCRs, they're a good investment. You can also observe transitions at various competitions, but it's much more difficult to remember them this way, as opposed to being able to play a routine back time and time again on the VCR.

A lot of novice bodybuilders get carried away and do far too many shots in a free-posing routine. In 60 seconds, they might do 20 shots—10 of which allow them to display their physique quite well, and 10 which make them look like the rookies they are. It's far better to do a 10-pose routine and look great all the way through.

As a final piece of advice, learn to get along without the mirror. (This goes for the other two posing rounds, as well.) Obviously, you have to spend a lot of time in front of the mirror when you're working on new poses, but you won't be able to look in one when you're competing onstage. So, get used to the idea of posing without that mirror as a crutch. This would be a good time to use videotaping equipment if you have it, since it also allows you to hear the sound of your music in synchronization with your poses—just as the judges or audience will do at a bodybuilding competition.

Confidence is a big plus onstage at a competition. It manifests as a winning look, so it's something you will definitely want to have. The easiest way to foster self-confidence is to have a lot of confidence in your ability to effectively display your physique—and that comes from plenty of posing practice!

From the posedown at the '88 Ms. Olympia. To the left is Cory Everson, with Anja Langer behind her.

The Posedown

The top five competitors after the three-round prejudging are entered in the posedown towards the end of each competition. This posedown will give you a final chance to gain a few crucial points, which might put you over the top competitively. Many shows have been won or lost during the posedown.

You should have an actual mini free-posing routine ready for each posedown, preferably one that includes only your best eight to 10 shots. Most bodybuilders go into a posedown totally unprepared, winging it according to what other competitors are doing. It's much better to have a set routine prepared to the point where you can do it both smoothly and enthusiastically.

Strategically, it's better if you can draw your competitors towards you to match or attempt to better your posedown shots. Don't allow them to pull you over into a one-on-one competition of best poses, because then it will look like you feel you're chasing them, something the judges notice right away. It's better to have your competition coming after you because they *know* you're winning.

In the midst of our final posedown at the '88 Ms. Olympia, five time Ms. Olympia Cory Everson and I engage in an impromptu arm-wrestling match.

ONSTAGE PERSONAL APPEARANCE

In close competitions, having a personal appearance that conveys a professional attitude can win a show for you. Therefore, it's very important to give some consideration to suit choice and onstage grooming.

You probably already have a good sense of which colors look best on you, but suit cut is another matter. The cut of your suit should be chosen to emphasize strong points and hide weaker areas. If you have great upper-thigh and hip flexor muscularity, the legs of your suit bottom should be cut up relatively high; if you don't have it, the cut should be lower. With great lower-ab muscularity, you'll look best with a suit bottom cut a little lower at the top; without it, be sure the suit comes up as high as possible to cover that area.

When choosing a suit top, try to find one that displays the most physical development, unless you have no chest muscularity at all and need to hide the fact. Sometimes you will need a different size for the bottom and the top, but most gyms and bodybuilding pro shops where you can buy posing suits will allow this, since it happens all the time.

You will undoubtedly have to try on several different types of suits in order to find one that both fits perfectly and has the right cut for your unique body. Once you find it, buy at least two suits—one for the prejudging and one for the night show—in case the first one gets spotted with oil or otherwise soiled.

Your hairstyle should be chosen to also accentuate your muscular development. This means putting longer hair up off your shoulders, where it won't hide your upper-back and shoulder development. Don't wear a hairstyle that's too severe, however, since it can detract from your femininity. A nice, soft perm works well for most women.

Onstage makeup must be heavier than normal, or the stage lights will wash it out. If you have any questions about how heavy it should be, try to attend a competition and get a peek at some of the women backstage warming up; then adjust your makeup accordingly for your own initial competition. Or, you can have a friend in the audience tell you whether you need to add more makeup or use less.

Your personal appearance will no doubt evolve at about the same rate as your physique. It's best to regard your first few contests primarily as part of your learning process (although you'll probably place well if you're suitably prepared). Use them to evaluate your physique, posing techniques, and personal appearance.

THE PUBLICITY EFFORT

As you rise in the bodybuilding ranks, you should try to gain some recognition by having your photos (eventually with accompanying stories) published in various bodybuilding magazines. For most bodybuilders, this is a daunting proposition at first, but you'll find it relatively easy to accomplish if you follow the suggestions in this section.

Once you're good enough, the bodybuilding press will come to you. But you'll usually have to be competing at a relatively high national level in order to attract this type of attention. During your first couple years of competition, you'll have to come up with publishable material on your own and send it to the magazines yourself.

Experienced and well-known bodybuilding photographers (like Mike Neveux, who took most of the photos in this book) consistently take the best physique and training photos. If such a photographer lives in your area, you may be able to talk him or her into taking photos of you. You might have to pay for the photographic work, but it will be worth the expense if the work gets into one of the magazines.

Even without having access to an established physique photographer, you can still get good photos if you have a friend or family member who owns a good-quality 35 mm. camera with a focusable lens. All you need to do is follow these simple rules for good outdoor physique photography:

• For color film, choose Kodak's Ektachrome 64 (with an ASA rating of 64), which produces color slides. For the best black-and-white photos, choose Kodak's Plus X film (ASA 125). Both types of film comes with 36 exposures to a roll.

• Choose a day in which you have either direct sunlight or sunlight lightly filtered through haze. The best angle of the sun on your body is about 45°, which means that summertime pics should be taken between 8 and 9 a.m., or between 3:30 and 4:30 p.m. But don't stand facing directly towards the sun. Rather, you should have it off at about a 20 to 30° angle from dead-on your face.

• Choose the most monotonous background possible. The best backgrounds are either the beach with water in the rear view, or merely the sky (which can be achieved by standing on a hill or rock and having the camera set at about knee height). Avoid buildings, bushes, or utility poles sprouting out of your head or body, and so forth. When at the beach, keep onlookers out of the photos, because they will distract attention away from you.

• Your body should be lightly oiled and as perfectly prepared as possible. If you don't have a dark skin tone, be sure you either have a natural tan or one out of the bottle.

• A relatively fast shutter speed on the camera should be used—preferably $1/500$th of a second ($1/250$th is also good, as long as the camera is held very still as the shutter is

Steve and I have a good time at Mike Neveux's photography studio when we're in Los Angeles. Mike took many of the photos in this book, and he's the best all-around physique photographer I know.

One of the best ways of constantly updating my knowledge of the sport is by reading bodybuilding magazines.

tripped). Regardless of the shutter speed chosen, the lens aperture should be appropriate for that shutter speed. (This is something that any experienced photographer can easily determine, but use the automatic setting on the camera should there be any doubt.) When using color film, try to have three pics of each pose shot—one at the metered setting, one a half stop below that, and one a half stop above. This will ensure a correct exposure on the more highly sensitive color film. (For black-and-white, you can actually miss the exposure by a full stop or more, since it can be corrected in the processing lab.)

• Have the photographer give you a count of three, tripping the shutter at three, so that you can be completely into your pose and have an appropriate facial expression in the photograph. If you doubt that you've gotten your stance correct, have another snap taken of the same pose.

• Once a couple of rolls have been shot, have them processed by a good lab. Color film can be sent on request to Kodak's own lab, which ensures the best possible processing. Black-and-white film should be sent to an actual photo processing lab, rather than being machine-developed, which is what happens with film you drop off at a drugstore or at one of those cute little huts in supermarket parking lots. With black-and-white film, have a proof sheet made up, from which you can choose frames to be enlarged. All enlargements *must* be hand-printed on 8 × 10–inch paper.

• Mount your transparencies (only the best ones) in plastic display sheets, which can be purchased at all photography stores.

When you have a good group of photos, select a magazine to send them to, and package them correctly, with sufficient return postage clipped to the photos. If you don't send in the postage, the magazine is under no obligation to return unused pictures to you. Be sure to use a large enough envelope to allow cardboard backing sheets to totally protect your photos.

I suggest beginning with the lower-level magazines, and then working upwards as your photos continue to be published in each succeeding level of magazine. Don't expect to get into *Flex* the first time you have photos taken. Instead, go for magazines that tend to publish pictures of the people against whom you're competing. Find the name of the magazine editor on the magazine's masthead, and then address your package directly to him or her. If your photos are good enough, they'll be published; if not, keep trying.

If a magazine editor takes a real interest in you, he or she may assign a local writer to do a story on you. Or, you can supply notes about yourself and your training and dietary methods, from which a staff writer can put together a story. Once you have that first story under your belt, start looking for a magazine a little higher up the ladder.

INFORMATION SOURCES

It's important for you to know as much as possible about your sport. Books like this are a good starting point, but you'll be frozen in time if you depend solely on books. To constantly update your information, you should read all the bodybuilding magazines, watching the newsstands for the latest issues. And you should seek contact with better bodybuilders, who always seem to know what's new in the sport.

If you work out in a major gym, you should have no trouble finding top bodybuilders with whom to talk. Just be sure that you wait until they are done working out before you approach them with your questions. Or, you can attend bodybuilding seminars, being certain to come to each with a list of questions you want to ask the champions. Often, you can get the most valuable information on the sport towards the end of a seminar, when the champion is answering questions from the audience, rather than giving a prepared presentation.

Always seek knowledge—with it, you'll make the most of your genetic potential, your self-discipline, and your hard work. Knowledge will make you a great champion in its own right. Go for it!

APPENDIX:

MY FAVORITE RECIPES

Guide to Approximate Equivalents

Customary			Metric		
Ounces Pounds	Cups	Table- spoons	Tea- spoons	Milli- litres	Grams Kilograms
			¼ t.	1 mL	1 g
			½ t.	2 mL	
			1 t.	5 mL	
			2 t.	10 mL	
½ oz.		1 T.	3 t.	15 mL	15 g
1 oz.		2 T.	6 t.	30 mL	30 g
2 oz.	¼ c.	4 T.	12 t.	60 mL	
4 oz.	½ c.	8 T.	24 t.	125 mL	
8 oz.	1 c.	16 T.	48 t.	250 mL	
2.2 lb.					1 kg

Keep in mind that this guide does not show exact conversions, but it can be used in a general way for food measurement.

Oven-Cooking Guide

Fahrenheit °F	Oven Heat	Celsius °C
250–275°	very slow	120–135°
300–325°	slow	150–165°
350–375°	moderate	175–190°
400–425°	hot	200–220°
450–475°	very hot	230–245°
475–500°	hottest	250–290°

OFF-SEASON

Caraway Slaw

2 cups finely shredded green cabbage
½ cup cottage cheese (1% maximum fat by weight)
¼ cup skimmed buttermilk, or slightly more if needed
1 8 oz. can unsweetened crushed pineapple, juice packed and drained
1 tablespoon white sugar or 1 pkt. Sweet 'n Low
1 teaspoon caraway seeds

Place the cabbage in a bowl of ice water to crisp. Blend the cottage cheese and buttermilk in a blender until very smooth, adding a little more buttermilk, if necessary. Transfer the blended mixture to a bowl and stir in the pineapple and seasonings. Chill well. Drain the cabbage thoroughly in a colander and stir into the chilled dressing.

Makes 3 to 4 servings

Calories: 67 for each fourth of recipe

Turkey Balls in Tomato Sauce

1 pound raw deboned turkey breast, or turkey breast slices, ground
1½ cups whole-wheat bread crumbs
1 cup finely chopped onions
¾ cup finely chopped green peppers
½ cup grated carrots
1 cup canned tomato juice
¼ cup frozen concentrated apple juice
1 teaspoon cider vinegar
1 teaspoon ground sage

Tomato Sauce:
3 cups tomato juice
4 tablespoons canned tomato paste
½ cup water
1 large apple, peeled and coarsely chopped
⅓ cup sherry
dash cayenne pepper

Combine all ingredients for the turkey balls in a bowl, mixing well. Shape into balls about 1½ inches in diameter and place them on a nonstick cookie sheet. Bake in a 400°F oven for about 30 minutes. To remove the turkey balls from the sheet, pour about ¼ cup of water around the balls onto the sheet and wait 2 to 3 minutes; then loosen with a spatula and transfer to a baking dish, arranging them in a single layer.

Sauce: Place the tomato products in a saucepan. Combine the apple with ½ cup water in a blender, and blend well until smooth; add the sherry and pepper, and blend. Then add this blended mixture to the saucepan, stir, and bring to a boil. Reduce heat and simmer over medium-to-low heat for 10 minutes, stirring as necessary. Pour the sauce over the turkey balls and bake, uncovered, in a 375°F oven for 20 minutes. Serve over whole-wheat pasta or white rice.

Yield: about 36 turkey balls with sauce
Calories: 165 for each four turkey balls and ½ cup of sauce
Poultry: 2 ounces for 4 turkey balls and ¼ cup sauce

Boston Baked Beans

2 cups dried navy beans
1 onion, chopped
⅔ cup canned tomato paste
½ cup canned tomato juice
¼ cup apple concentrate
¼ cup white wine
¼ cup water
2 tablespoons cider vinegar
1 teaspoon grated ginger
1 teaspoon dry mustard
¼ teaspoon garlic powder
¼ teaspoon ground cloves
⅛ teaspoon cardamom
dash cayenne pepper

Place the beans in a pot and add water enough to cover (about 5 cups). Bring the water to a boil, reduce heat, and cook the beans for 5 to 10 minutes. Turn off the heat, cover, and let the beans soak for an hour. Return to a boil, and cook over a moderate heat, with the cover ajar, until the beans are tender (it takes about an hour). Stir occasionally to prevent sticking. Add a little water towards the end of the cooking period, if the beans seem to be dry. Measure off 4 cups of beans and mix them with all the other ingredients. Pour that bean mixture off into a casserole, cover, and return to a 350°F oven for about an hour.

Yield: about 5 cups Calories: 130 per half-cup

My Favorite White Chocolate Chip Cookies

¾ cup whole-wheat flour
⅜ cup protein powder
⅛ cup bran
⅔ cup soft butter or margarine
½ teaspoon baking soda
¾ cup brown sugar
1 teaspoon water
½ teaspoon vanilla extract
1 egg
1 cup (6 oz.) white chocolate, in chunks or chips

Sift and mix together flour, protein powder, bran, and baking soda. Combine butter, sugar, water, and vanilla, mixing well. Beat in egg. Add flour mixture, mix well. Then stir in chocolate. Drop by one-teaspoonful pieces onto lightly greased baking sheets. Bake at 375°F for 10 to 12 minutes, or until lightly browned.

Back-To-Nature Bread

1 cup golden raisins
1¾ cups water
⅓ cup shortening
3 packets active dry yeast
1 cup whole-wheat pastry flour
pinch salt
⅓ cup wheat germ
⅓ cup brown sugar
½ teaspoon ginger
½ teaspoon cinnamon
2 cups whole-wheat flour
1 cup all-purpose flour

Combine raisins, 1¼ cups water, and shortening. Heat to boiling, stirring until shortening melts. Remove from heat and cool to lukewarm. Soften yeast in remaining ½ cup water. Add sugar, salt, spices, and cup of whole-wheat pastry flour, and mix well. Add raisin mixture. Gradually mix in remaining flours and wheat germ. Turn out onto a well-floured board and knead 3 minutes. Return to mixing bowl, and brush top of dough with oil. Cover and let rise until doubled, about 1¾ hours. Punch down and shape into a loaf. Place into a greased pan (9 x 3 x 5″) and brush top with oil. Let rise until doubled, about 45 minutes. Bake in lower part of oven at about 375°F for 40 minutes or until nicely browned. Turn out onto wire rack to cool. Makes a large loaf.

PRECONTEST

Garlic Broiled Chicken

1 white chicken breast, halved and skinned

Basting sauce:
½ teaspoon garlic, minced
1 tablespoon lemon juice
½ teaspoon lemon pepper
1 teaspoon Dijon mustard

Combine all basting ingredients. Brush over chicken. Broil 10 minutes each side, brushing frequently with sauce.

Makes 1–2 servings

Chicken and Rice Soup

2 full chicken breasts
1 medium onion, quartered
1 large carrot, sliced
2 cloves garlic
2 quarts water
2 stalks celery, sliced
1 teaspoon oregano
1 large bay leaf
pepper
½ cup brown rice
2 medium carrots, diced
3 tablespoons parsley

Put chicken, onion, carrot, and garlic in a large pot and cover with cold water. Bring to a boil; then add oregano, bay leaf, and pepper to taste. Reduce heat to simmer and cook, uncovered, until chicken is very tender, about 2 hours. Strain off broth, cool or refrigerate, and skim off fat. Now, return skimmed broth to pot with chicken, which has been divided into small pieces, and bring to a boil. Add rice and simmer, covered, for 25 minutes. Then add carrots, celery, and parsley. Simmer another 10 minutes. (Additional ingredients can be included, such as 1 medium zucchini, diced, and 1 cup of fresh or frozen peas and/or corn.)

Makes 6–8 servings

Corn Bread

1½ cups whole-grain yellow cornmeal
¾ cup whole-wheat pastry flour
1 tablespoon baking powder
1 teaspoon baking soda
1 teaspoon onion powder
1 cup skimmed buttermilk
¼ cup frozen apple juice concentrate
3 egg whites

Combine dry ingredients, stirring to mix well. Stir in the other ingredients, except the egg whites. Beat the egg whites until soft peaks form; then fold them into the batter. Transfer to a nonstick 8x10 in. baking pan, and bake, uncovered, for 20 minutes in a 400°F oven. Remove from oven and cover pan with foil. Allow to cool; then cut into squares.

Yields 16 squares   78 calories/square

Blueberry Jam

1 teaspoon unflavored gelatin (or 1½–2 teaspoons for a thicker jam)
⅓ cup bottled white grape juice
1 tablespoon lemon juice
1 12-ounce package frozen unsweetened blueberries, or 2¼ cups fresh blueberries

Sprinkle gelatin over 2 tablespoons of grape juice to soften. Place the rest of the grape juice with the other ingredients in a saucepan. Stir and cook over moderate heat for about 5 minutes or until the blueberries are thick and crushed. Stir in the softened gelatin and cook over low heat until dissolved. Allow to cool; then store in a covered jar in the refrigerator or freezer.

44 calories/¼ cup

Clam Sauce for Pasta

1 packet of Butterbuds
1 large clove garlic, finely minced
1 tablespoon finely chopped parsley, or 1 teaspoon dried parsley
½ cup hot water
2 6½ oz. cans clams, drained

Dissolve Butterbuds in hot water. Add garlic and drained clams. Heat to simmer. Add parsley. Serve over cooked pasta.

Vegetable Curry

2 sliced onions
⅓ cup vegetable or chicken stock
1½ tablespoons curry powder
½ tablespoon soy sauce
2 tablespoons chopped cumin
dash cayenne pepper
1 eggplant, peeled and chopped
3 carrots, thinly sliced
1 green pepper, sliced
3 garlic cloves, minced
3 chopped tomatoes
⅓ cup raisins
2 tablespoons tomato paste
½ cup frozen peas, rinsed

In a large skillet, dry-sauté onions over moderate heat until softened; then remove from skillet and set aside. Bring stock to a boil in skillet, reduce heat, and stir in curry powder, soy sauce, cumin, and cayenne pepper. Add the carrots, green pepper, and garlic. Return to a boil; then lower heat to moderate, and stirring frequently, cook for about 15 minutes or until vegetables are tender. Stir in tomatoes, raisins, and tomato paste. Cover and simmer for 5 minutes, stirring occasionally. Mix in onions and green peas, and heat thoroughly.

Makes 5 servings, 159 calories per serving

Oat-Wheat-Rice Pancakes

2 cups water
1½ cups regular rolled oats
1 cup whole-wheat pastry flour
¼ cup frozen apple juice concentrate
2 heaping tablespoons cooked brown rice
1 tablespoon baking powder
1½ teaspoons vanilla extract
2 egg whites, beaten until stiff

Combine all of the ingredients, except the egg whites, in a blender and blend until smooth. Fold in the egg whites. Heat a nonstick skillet to a moderate temperature or until a drop of water will dance over the surface. Pour the batter into the skillet to make pancakes of desired size. Bake until bubbles form on the top and the underside is browned; then flip over and bake until the other side is equally browned. Serve with a sprinkling of cinnamon and unsweetened applesauce, or other low-calorie sweet topping.

Yields: 2 to 4 servings   253 calories/quarter recipe

Apple-Oat-Bran Muffins

4 egg whites, lightly beaten
¾ cup nonfat milk
½ cup nonfat yogurt
¼ cup frozen apple juice concentrate
1 cup regular rolled oats
1 cup bran
2 apples, peeled and grated
½ cup raisins, or chopped and pitted dates (optional)
1½ cups whole-wheat pastry flour
1½ teaspoons baking soda
1 teaspoon cinnamon

Combine eggs, milk, yogurt, apple juice, oats, and bran, and stir to mix lightly. Stir in apples and raisins (or dates, if used). In a separate bowl, combine flour, baking soda, and cinnamon, stirring to mix well. Add the dry ingredients to the fruit mixture, stirring lightly to combine well. Spoon into nonstick muffin pans and bake in a 425°F oven for 25 minutes.

Yield: about 24 muffins 67 calories per muffin

INDEX

A

Abdominals, basic and isolation exercises, 70
Alcohol, 85
Amino-acid supplements, 95
Apple-oat bran muffins, 158

B

Back
   basic and isolation exercises, 70
   trisets for, 123
Back double-biceps pose, 142–143
Back-to-nature bread, 156
Barbell curls, standing, 33
Barbell presses, incline
   progression for, 20
Basal metabolic rate (BMR), 134
Basic exercises, 70
Basile, Vince, 11
B-complex vitamins, 87
Behind-neck pulldowns, 107–108
Belts, 128
Bench press, 18, 19
   close-grip, 34, 35
Bend-over rows, barbell, 46, 47
Biceps, basic and isolation exercises, 70
Biofeedback, 129
Biomechanics, 24, 26
BMR (basal metabolic rate), 134
Bodybuilding, eclectic, 136
Bodybuilding magazines, 153
Body wraps, 128–129
Boston baked beans, 155
Bread recipes, 156–157
Breathing patterns, 26

C

Cable bent-over laterals, 44, 45
Calf raises
   donkey, 40
   seated, 37
   standing, 36
Calves, basic and isolation exercises, 70
Caraway slaw, 154
Carbohydrate depletion-loading, 90, 92, 95
Carbohydrates, 87
Cheating reps, 26, 63
Chest
   basic and isolation exercises, 70
   trisets for, 123
Chicken and rice soup, 157
Chins, 74, 75
Clam sauce for pasta, 158
Close-grip lat pulldowns, 126, 127
Compulsory poses, 141–144
Concentration, 107–108
Confidence, 147
Continuous tension, 122–123
Corn bread, 157
Crunch, 38, 39, 66
Cycle-dieting principle, 85–86

D

Deadlifts, 30, 31
Deltoids, trisets, 123
DeMilia, Wayne, 16
Dennis, Diana, 16
Descending sets, 116
Diary, training, 130, 131
Dips, parallel bar, 42, 43
Donkey calf raises, 40
Double-split routines, 134, 136
Dumbbell presses, incline, 76, 77

E

Enthusiasm, 108, 111
Everson, Cory, 138, 148, 149
Exercise(s), 18
   basic and isolation, 70
   poundages for, 23

F

Fats, dietary, 85, 89–90
Food supplements, 85, 87, 94, 95, 96, 97
Forced reps, 46, 63–64
Forearms, basic and isolation exercises, 70
Form, correct, 24, 26
Francis, Bev, 9–11, 13
   personal meal plans of, 96–97
Free weights, vs. machines, 69
Front abdominal-and-thigh pose, 143–144
Front double-biceps pose, 141–142
Full-pyramid, 72

G

Garlic broiled chicken, 157
Giant sets, 123–124
Goal-setting process, 102, 105, 106
Gyms, commercial vs. home, 23

H

Hairstyle, 150
Half-pyramid, 72
Hanging leg raises, 24, 25
Holistic training, 69, 72

I

Incline barbell presses, progression for, 20
Incline dumbbell presses, 76, 77
Information sources, 153
Injuries, 64, 66–67
Inspiration, 108, 111
Isolation exercises, 70
Iso-tension, 136, 138

J

Jam, blueberry, 157

L

Leg extensions, 68, 123
Leg press, 27
Leg raises, hanging, 24, 25
Legs
   basic and isolation exercises, 70
   trisets for, 123
Long-range goals, 102
Lower guide number, 19

M

Machines, vs. free weights, 69
Makeup, 150
Mass-building process, 48
Measurement equivalents, 154
Mental visualization drills, 111, 113
Mind power, 100, 113
Muffins, apple-oat bran, 158
Muscle-confusion technique, 78
Muscle hypertrophy, 18–21
Muscle priority, 58, 62

N

Neck flexing, 137
Neck machine, 2-way, 17
Negative thought journal, 101
Nutrition, 82, 85
   cycle-dieting principle, 85–86
   off-season diet, 87
   precontest diet, 89–90

O

Oat-wheat-rice pancakes, 158
Off-season diet, 96
   recipes for, 154–156
Oliva, Sergio, 11
Overtraining, 50, 67–68

P

Palyo, Cathey, 140
Parallel bar dips, 42, 43
Peak contraction, 119, 121
Personal appearance, onstage, 150

Photography, 150–151, 153
Physical exams, 23
Plateaus, breaking, 78
Posedown, 148
Posing, 138–149
Posing rounds
  one, 138, 139, 141–144
  two, 145
  three, 145–147
Positive thinking, 100–101
Potential, for bodybuilding, 56, 58
Power bodybuilding, 42–43, 51
Preacher curl, one-arm dumbbell, 21
Precontest diet, 96, 119
Precontest water balancing, 90, 92, 95
Pre-exhaustion supersets, 74–75
Presses behind neck, on Smith machine, 52, 53
Program, 19
Progression, 18–20
Progressive resistance exercise, 18
Publicity effort, 150–151, 153
Public relations, 134
Pulldowns
  behind-neck, 107–108
  close-grip lat, 126, 127
Pulley push-downs, 125
Pulse rate, 68
Push-downs, pulley, 125
Pyramiding, 72

Q

Quality training, 116, 119

R

Ragain, Janice, 140
Recipes, 154–158
Reinforcement straps, 32
Repetitions, 18, 43
Rest and recovery, 67–69
Rest intervals, 18, 23–24, 119
Reverse curls, 57
Rewards of bodybuilding, 16
RICE, 64
Routines
  beginning level, for conditioning, 33
  changing, 26
  double-split, 134, 136
  individualizing, 78–79
  intermediate level, for conditioning, 33
  power-bodybuilding, 51
  split, 73
Ruberts, Winston, 16

S

Salt, 85
Schwarzenegger, Arnold, 10
Seated pulley rows, 48, 49
Selectorized weight stacks, 117, 118
Self-actualization, 111
Self-confidence, 50, 111, 113
Set(s), 18–19
  descending, 116
  for various experience levels, 67
Shoes, 26
Short-range goals, 105–106
Shoulders, basic and isolation exercises, 70
Shrugs, 86
Side chest pose, 142
Side laterals, dumbbell, 50–51
Side triceps pose, 143
Sodium-loading depletion, 90, 92
Soup, chicken and rice, 157
Split routine, 62, 73
Squat, 60–62
Straps, reinforcement, 32
Supersets, 73–74
  pre-exhaustion, 74–75, 78

T

Thought process in training, 13
Training ability, instinctive, 129
Training diary, 130, 131
Training intensity, increasing, 63–64
Training partners, 26, 28
Training poundages, 119
Triceps, basic and isolation exercises, 70
Trisets, 123–124
Turkey balls in tomato sauce, 155

U

Upper guide number, 19

V

Van Maris, Ellen, 140
Vegetable curry, 158
Visualization, mental, 111, 113
Vitamins, 87, 94

W

Warm-ups, 28
Water
  drinking of, 82
  precontest balancing, 90, 92, 95
Weightlifting belt, 128
Weinberger, Steve, 11, 16, 22
White chocolate chip cookies, 156
Women, 48, 50
Working wear, 26
Wraps, 128–129